JEREMY SIEPMANN

The Piano

EVERYMAN'S LIBRARY–EMI CLASSICS
MUSIC COMPANIONS

Front endpaper: The Pleyel Factory in Paris (Mary Evans Picture
Library).
Back endpaper: View of the action room in the Chickering Piano
Manufactory, Tremont Street, Boston, in 1887 (Culver Pictures Inc.,
New York).
Title page: Extract from Mozart's written out Cadenza for his Piano
Concerto no. 9 in E flat, K271.
Page ii: A 19th-century giraffe piano (Sotheby's).
Page vi: An Erard grand piano *c.* 1840 (Copyright © The
Metropolitan Museum of Art. Gift of Mrs. Henry McSweeny, 1959.
[59.76]).

Series General Editor: Michael Rose

Picture research by Helen Ottaway

Typeset in the UK by AccComputing, Castle Cary, Somerset
Printed and bound in Germany by Mohndruck Graphische Betriebe
GmbH, Gütersloh

Contents

Preface

This book is what it says it is: a companion. It is not, strictly speaking, a history. It is neither a narrative nor a reference book, though it contains elements of both. It lays no claim to being comprehensive in its coverage (no book of its size could hope to do that), but its range is wide. Its organization, for the most part, is generic rather than chronological, and the emphasis throughout is on the musical and social rather than the technical and economic. Readers wanting more detailed information on the mechanical development and marketing of the piano can turn with confidence to Professor Cyril Ehrlich's admirably thorough but concise *The Piano: A History* and to Rosamond Harding's pioneering work, *The Pianoforte: Its History Traced to the Great Exhibition of 1851.*

An essential feature of the Everyman–EMI Music Companions is the inclusion with each volume of three compact discs, relieving much of the frustration normally experienced by writers on music and adding immeasurably to the reader's experience. I have largely let the music speak for itself, but where the performers concerned are generally conceded to have been among the greatest pianists of the century, I have included biographical sketches, either in the main body of the text or, where such episodes would have impeded the continuity of the narrative, in an Appendix at the end of the book. With one exception, Chapter 5 is devoted exclusively to great pianists of the nineteenth century, whose art was never (or never reliably) captured by recording. That one exception is Paderewski, who lived and recorded well into the twentieth century, but whose story belongs properly to the nineteenth (the calendar being no respecter of history: effectively, the nineteenth century came to an end only with the outbreak of the First World War in 1914). Because limits have to be drawn somewhere, I have chosen not to discuss pianists who are still before the public at the time of writing.

Let the Pianola Piano bring you happiness in 1914.

Do not merely hope for increased happiness in the year that is before you—ensure it by purchasing a Pianola Piano. There is no other investment you can make which will so surely bring pleasure to you and every member of your household, for by its means everyone can play the music they love. Day in, day out, through many a year the influence of the world's sweetest music will brighten and cheer you through the dull routine of life.

The Pianola Piano is the genuine Pianola combined with the **STEINWAY, WEBER, STECK,** or **STROUD** Piano. You are invited to play at Æolian Hall, or to write for Illustrated Catalogue " J."

THE ORCHESTRELLE COMPANY, ÆOLIAN HALL,

135-6-7, New Bond Street, LONDON, W.

CHAPTER 1

The Acorn and the Oak

There was hardly a bar in the Western world without one. No brothel, no stately home, no Sunday school. No picture palace worthy of the name, no ocean liner, no lumber camp, no town hall, no five-and-dime emporium. The 'pianna' was ubiquitous (west of the Mississippi in the United States one still occasionally hears it pronounced 'pie-anna'). Back in the 1790s, most people had never seen, much less heard one. Before 50 years had passed, however, England alone boasted 300 firms, disgorging more than 20,000 instruments a year. Throughout the nineteenth century, piano sales in Europe increased at a greater rate than the population. English, French and German makers dispatched battalions of pianos to every corner of the earth: to Southern and Eastern Europe, to Russia, Latin America, Australia, South Africa, India, Japan, the Philippines, to Borneo and Bali, to Delhi and Helsinki. Pianos were loaded onto the backs of camels for dispersal throughout Arabia. On 29 November 1856, a letter from Constantinople appeared in the *New York Musical Review and Gazette,* affirming that 'very few harems are now without a

Delivery of a Steinway to India at the turn of the century.

pianoforte, and many of the Turkish ladies are excellent performers'. If you hankered to learn the piano and happened to live in Paris in 1868, you had more than 20,000 piano teachers to choose from, without once leaving the city limits. And yet the pinnacle of the instrument's popularity had still not been achieved. Four decades later, the United States had established supremacy in the industry and was turning out, and selling, more than 350,000 pianos a year.

Hardly less remarkable, in its way, was the incendiary effect of certain famed virtuosos, whose matadorial flair at the keyboard occasionally provoked such hysteria that the police had to be summoned. One player was accompanied through the streets of a European capital by a torchlit parade of thousands; another traversed the United States in his own private railway carriage, attended by a team of acolytes which would have embarrassed a president, and emerging now and again to wave his benediction to the throngs that had gathered to see him pass by. Others appealed to a more discriminating coterie. When the twentieth century was already well advanced, a distinguished Hungarian played an entire recital, and for a capacity audience, on a piano from which the hammers had been entirely removed – a surgical feat of ineffable elegance when contrasted with another concert, of still later date, at which the performer, on the specific instructions of the 'composer', hacked a piano to bits with an axe.

Had the latter act taken place in mid-nineteenth-century Paris, London, Hamburg or New York, its perpetrator would have been lucky to escape with his life. It is difficult for us today to understand the degree to which the piano was itself an object of worship. Born in the twilight of the traditional master craftsman, it grew to maturity as one of the commercial and technological triumphs of the Industrial Revolution. Merely as a machine, with its hundreds of factory-made parts, combining the exotic substances of ivory and ebony with iron, steel and copper, it was revered, not least as a bountiful source of employment. As a symbol of the Romantic Age, with its glorification of man over nature and of science over God, it had extraordinary potency. Simply to own a piano was almost universally perceived as a badge of respectability.

Importantly, too, it was a child of the housebound north, where extended families and their friends were thrown together in confined surroundings by long and bitter winter nights. Prior to the advent of domestic electricity and such later and liberating developments as the radio, the record player and the automobile, the piano served, at almost every level of society, as a focal point of entertainment and an efficacious social lubricant. Indeed it proved amongst the middle classes an invaluable aid on the road to the altar, and to bed. It is a demonstrable fact that no musical instrument, including the ostensibly 'romantic' violin, has ever matched the power of the piano as an aphrodisiac. Or as a sales ploy. From the beginning, or very nearly, the piano and big business have walked hand in hand.

No instrument, not even the organ, that most extravagant of music machines, has proved so irresistible, or so inspiring, to the compulsive tinkerer. The range and ingenuity of the gadgetry lavished upon it is a story in itself.

But have we not left something out? Is there not one primary function of the piano we have omitted to discuss? The names of Bach or Mozart have not yet been raised, nor those of Beethoven, Schubert, Chopin, Liszt, Brahms, Debussy or Ravel. In the story of the piano, they have played a major part – though not so major as the likes of Badarzewska, Herz and Gottschalk, let alone Stephen Foster, František Kotzwara and Ethelbert Nevin. The piano is, after all, a musical instrument – perhaps the greatest ever made. In its versatility and range, in the breadth and quality of its repertoire, in the subtlety of its imagery and the grandeur of its sound, it has no rivals. More great music, and more bad music, has been composed for it than for any other instrument in history, from Beethoven's 32 sonatas ('The New Testament' of music, as Pablo Casals called them, distinguishing them from Bach's *Well-tempered Clavier*, 'The Old Testament') to the Debussy *Préludes* and the piano works of Messiaen; from *The Battle of Prague* and *The Maiden's Prayer* to the worst of contemporary hymns and the inane jingles that come as standard issue with the cheaper electronic keyboards (if we recognize these as a further stage in pianistic evolution).

*   *   *

By the middle of the eighteenth century, the piano was an idea whose time had come. The two domestic keyboard instruments which had ruled the roost for the last hundred years, the instruments of Bach, Handel and Scarlatti, were beset by increasingly frustrating limitations. The clavichord, with its touch-sensitive keyboard, was capable of extraordinary nuance but its sound was too small to project across a small room, let alone a concert hall. This sound, on the clavichord, was produced by a striker (or tangent, to give it its proper name) which remained in contact with the string and therefore allowed the player a degree of control over volume and phrasing. The plucked action of the harpsichord, on the other hand, meant that the player had no way of affecting the sound once it had been produced – or indeed of modifying the impact on the string in the first place. The only way of varying the volume on a harpsichord was the purely mechanical one of changing 'stops' or changing keyboards, rather as on an organ, and there was little opportunity for the kind of phrasing or nuance in which the clavichord excelled. Even at the apex of its development, the clavichord remained essentially a player's instrument ('that thrilling confidante of solitude', one writer called it), and if the harpsichord, by contrast, had the requisite power, it entirely lacked the clavichord's expressive, almost song-like suppleness of line. What was needed was an instrument combining the virtues of both with none of their attendant disadvantages.

With a synchronicity strangely common in the history of creative endeavour, the piano was invented, more or less simultaneously, and as far as we know, quite independently, by three different men in three different countries, at a time (very early in the eighteenth century) when communications between one centre and another were still primitive by modern standards. But for the 'idea' of the piano, we must look still further into the past.

On the periphery of mainstream musical traditions there have always been musical entertainers who resist categorization; one might almost call them freaks – like the man whose dead-end speciality was playing on two horns at once, or the fiddler who made a whole career out of imitating cats, chickens and old women on his violin. In this eternal parade of oddities, there were some, though not many, who commanded real respect, and a still smaller minority who contributed significantly to the course of musical evolution.

One of these was a man whose curious name, Pantaleon Hebenstreit, found its way into the history books, and even, for a time, into the standard vocabulary of musical drawing-rooms. We encounter him first in Saxony, in the late 1690s, as an itinerant dancing master and violinist of no particular brilliance. Yet within less than a decade he was a coddled celebrity and a welcome house guest at the resplendent home of Louis XIV in France, and he ended his days at the royal court of Dresden, with a salary almost twice that paid to J. S. Bach 20 years later as Cantor of St Thomas's in Leipzig. It was neither his dancing nor his fiddling, however, that earned him his fame or his income, but his virtuosity on a unique instrument invented by himself.

During a period of unemployment in Saxony, Hebenstreit came across a small, crude instrument used in the homes of peasants and in taverns and commonly known as a 'Hackbrett' (literally, a hacking- or chopping-board). The instrument caught Hebenstreit's attention, and he set about improving it. What he ended up with was a kind of giant dulcimer, involving not one but two sounding-boards, each more than six feet long, over which were stretched some 200 strings encompassing a range of five and a half octaves and all the musical possibilities of the chromatic scale (comprising the 12 equidistant half-steps that lie within the span of an octave). He now developed a technique of playing it, using two sticks to strike the strings, each one covered by a different material so as to vary not only the volume produced but the tone quality. In his hands, the instrument became something uniquely thrilling. It was now far removed from the peasant's 'hacking-board' – indeed in power and responsiveness, in the sheer variety of tones it could produce, it anticipated the concert grand pianos of the nineteeenth and twentieth centuries. It also introduced something quite new into the experience of domestic listening. Witness this report of a performance at the home of Ninon de L'Enclos, a close friend of Louis XIV's:

> He [Hebenstreit] was granted an attention interrupted only by the applause he received from all those who listened to him, according to the degree of sensitivity that each one had for music. Among the others, one could follow on Mlle de L'Enclos's face the various movements and the different passions that the musician sought to express: for she found expression where we often found only harmony, and one could have said that for her every note was a feeling.

Every note 'a feeling'. That was the new element. Particularly in France, music had been seen as something essentially decorative, not

An early instrument by Cristofori, Florence, 1720.

as an emotional experience. But Hebenstreit (or Monsieur Pantaleon, as he became known) showed that on an instrument such as his, feeling and emotional excitement could be captured and conveyed with hardly less vividness than on the operatic stage. It was this fact, perhaps, more than any other that led to the eventual popularity of the piano, which could do the same and more. And to bear out the connection, it became common in many places, and long after Hebenstreit's death, to refer to the parlour piano as a 'pantaleon'.

In reacting as she did to Hebenstreit's super-chopping-board, Ninon de L'Enclos was reflecting something more than a purely personal response. In some respects she was merely evincing the spirit of her age – and it was an age ripe for change. The great French harpsichordist and composer François Couperin, writing in 1711, expressed a frustration that was becoming general.

> Although the harpsichord is perfect as to its compass, and brilliant in itself, it is yet impossible to swell out or diminish the volume of its sound. I shall therefore be forever grateful to anyone who by the exercise of infinite art supported by fine taste contrives to render this instrument capable of expression.

Unbeknown to Couperin, his dream had already been fulfilled. Two years or so earlier, in or around 1709, in Florence, the Italian harpsichord maker Bartolomeo Cristofori had constructed the world's first piano, though at the time he saw it not so much as a new instrument as the modification of an old one, hence his grandiloquent title 'gravicembalo col piano e forte' (literally, 'harpsichord with soft and loud').* In fact the modifications were far more significant than Cristofori's description. All but the most modest of harpsichords had the capacity to play both 'soft and loud', but only in stark juxtaposition. What made Cristofori's instrument unique was an ingenious mechanism which rendered the keys touch-sensitive, giving to the fingers the

---

*Although Cristofori was the first man actually to construct a piano as we know it today, it is interesting to note that experiments of a similar nature were undertaken in the Netherlands as much as a century earlier.

power of varying the loudness by means of varying speed and pressure. It says something for Cristofori's originality and genius that the essential principles of his invention remained the basis for all sub-sequent developments during the next hundred years. Yet strange though it may seem for a land which had been the cradle of both opera and the instrumental concerto, the earliest sounds of the most expressive keyboard instrument ever devised fell largely on deaf ears. To this day, Cristofori retains his position as both the first and the last great Italian piano maker. After an initial flurry of attention, and a set of 12 *Sonate da cimbalo di piano e forte detto volgarmente di martellati* by Lodovico Giustini (the first known music ever to be composed expressly for the new instrument),* the Italians turned their backs on the piano for the best part of 200 years. It would be wrong to imagine, however, that the sounds they heard then were more than remotely comparable to those of the humblest upright, let alone a modern grand. Well into the eighteenth century, the piano was closer in sound and construction to the harpsichord than to the instrument we know today. The strings were both fewer and thinner, the frame of the instrument was of wood, as with the harpsichord, and the hammers were both lighter and harder. Indeed, for some considerable time the piano was less brilliant, and less powerful in sound, than the biggest harpsichords of the time.

It was not in France or Italy, however, but in Germany that the piano struck its first significantly resonating chords. And again the time was ripe. Throughout much of the seventeenth and eighteenth centuries, Germany had been awash in a cult of 'feeling' that led straight to the first flowering of the Romantic movement, as exempli-fied in literature by Goethe and Schiller. What had begun as a religious movement known as Pietism, dedicated to the humanizing of Lutheran worship in the face of excessive theological dogma, had developed into a generalized worship of 'sensibility'. The small-toned but supremely touch-sensitive clavichord was much cultivated by the

*A facsimile edition was published by Cambridge University Press in 1933.

Pietists, who belonged mainly to the socially ascendant middle class; but as the eighteenth century wore on, the thrill of solitude increasingly gave way to the thrill of emotional exhibitionism. Public weeping became a badge of admirable sensitivity, especially among men, some of whom became lachrymose almost to the point of routine. Emotion was celebrated above logic, 'song' above 'form', 'humanity' above doctrine. The deficiencies of the organ and harpsichord as media for such expressive values grew increasingly irksome. What was needed to voice the determinedly warm humanity of this strongly family-based society was a keyboard instrument combining the melodic subtlety of the clavichord with the power and grandeur of the biggest harpsichords. The stage was thus set for the most spectacular and prolonged success in the entire history of instrumental endeavour. The explanation, however, lies at least as much with psychology and physiology as with history or sociology.

It is a well-established fact that variations of tonal intensity have immediate and often dramatic effects on the body's chemistry, and that these have a direct correlation with the physical manifestations of emotion (grief, euphoria, fear, sexual excitement, humour, etc.). A swift increase of tonal intensity is a powerful stimulant, with measurable and often dramatic effects on the nervous system. Sudden and unexpected blasts of sound can induce a state of shock which at its most extreme can prove fatal. A gradual increase of volume, on the other hand, can excite a state of pleasurable expectation, dilating the pupils of the eyes, inducing a delicate film of tears, expanding the facial capillaries, perhaps bringing a blush to the cheeks, and many other similar changes affecting circulation, heart rate, blood pressure, muscular tension, electrical activity in the brain and so on. Interestingly, these symptoms rely on the *variation* of the stimulus. Since the nervous system adapts so quickly to altered circumstances, any prolonged level of tone will soon lose much of its stimulant properties. Any instrument, therefore, which is restricted, like the clavichord, to a very narrow dynamic range, or confined, like the harpsichord, to a set number of inflexible dynamic levels, is correspondingly limited in the range of emotions it can embrace. The piano, on the other hand, can move smoothly from one dynamic extreme to another and encompass any number of contrasts in between. As an emotional generator it is in a class by itself.

The first great piano maker in Germany, Gottfried Silbermann, was himself no stranger to emotion, and was already renowned for his clavichords and organs. Silbermann, however, was very much more than a master craftsman. He had a shrewd head for business, a genius for publicity, a predatory obsession with the opposite sex and an incorrigible taste for practical jokes which once earned him the tenancy of a jail cell. In the tiny hamlet of his birth in Saxony on 14 January 1683, he had gulled some villagers into believing that a hoard of ancient treasure was buried in a nearby ruin and was theirs for the taking. Heavily armed with spades and shovels, they approached the spot at dead of night, tripping as intended over a carefully concealed rope and releasing a circular choir of hidden artillery – to the uproarious mirth of the perpetrator. If nothing else, the efficiency of the operation was a tribute to his ingenuity – as was his early escape from jail.

In 1709 he settled in Freiburg, from whence, however, his sexual escapades soon forced him to make a hasty exit. He then lodged for a time with his brother in distant Strasbourg, until a bungled attempt at abducting a nun forced his rapid departure from that city too. His notoriety and fame then advanced in tandem, his perfectionism becoming as legendary as his impatience. Known to have smashed a succession of church windows while searching for an irritating rattle, he demolished with an axe those of his instruments which failed to meet his exacting standards.

During his residence in Freiburg, Silbermann came to know the celebrated Hebenstreit, who was enjoying an Indian summer at the royal court in nearby Dresden. His unwieldy instrument, expensive and difficult to maintain at the best of times, was showing its age and urgently required the attentions of an expert craftsman. Silbermann fitted the bill to perfection and was later entrusted with the building of a replacement.

Grand piano by Gottfried Silbermann,
c. 1745 – one of three Silbermann pianos
belonging to Frederick the Great that
survived to this century.

In the course of playing nanny to the royal eccentric, Silbermann was inspired to some independent flights of fancy. While building a new pantaleon for its celebrated master, it occurred to him that the hammers need not be held in the two hands of the player but could rather be set in motion by ten fingers through the well-tried agency of a keyboard. At around the same time he made the acquaintance of a man who knew, at least by hearsay, of Cristofori's work in Italy.

In 1730, effectively 'borrowing' Cristofori's mechanism wholesale, he made the first piano ever to have been built in Germany. Six years later his handiwork was scrutinized by none other than Johann Sebastian Bach, whose criticisms – that the action was heavy and unreliable, and the tone of the treble too weak – evidently enraged him. On the great man's departure, Silbermann's axe was put through its customary paces, but the justice of Bach's comments could not be ignored.

Eleven years later, at the court of Frederick the Great in Potsdam, where his son Carl Philipp Emanuel had been in service since 1740, Bach encountered Silbermann's most recent instruments and now proclaimed himself well pleased. Given the grovelling tone of his dedication to Frederick of the *Musical Offering*, however, his praise should be taken with a grain of salt. Certainly he failed to put his music where his mouth was. Despite a brief and little-known fling as a piano salesman in 1749, he never showed the slightest interest in writing for the instrument. The claim that it is therefore 'wrong' to play Bach's music on the modern piano, which bears only a vestigial resemblance to its mid-eighteenth-century counterpart, is, however, a form of false piety. History apart, it can objectively and conclusively be demonstrated that today's piano, properly handled, is unsurpassed as a medium for Bachian polyphony.

Silbermann's renown, Frederick's custom and Bach's widely reported approbation did nothing to harm the piano's progress in Germany. By 1752, its superiority over the harpsichord and clavichord was being trumpeted by the highly esteemed Johann Joachim Quantz (with C. P. E. Bach, the most famous musician in Frederick's retinue) in one of the major treatises in musical history.* So closely was Silbermann's name associated with the instrument that he was commonly supposed to have invented it. Yet he was never a specialist. In addition to his many fine harpsichords, pianos and clavichords, he built 47 first-class organs in Saxony, where he died, unmarried but rich, in 1753.

Of the many musicians whose custom he had enjoyed, one stood out above all others in celebrity and influence alike. Indeed Carl Philipp Emanuel Bach, the second son of Johann Sebastian, enjoyed a fame in his lifetime all but eclipsing that of his father. Unchallenged as the most important German composer in the transition from the Baroque to the Classical era (and hence from the harpsichord to the piano), he was among the most distinguished performers of his time

---

* *Versuch einer Anweisung die Flöte traversiere zu spielen* (literally, Essay of an Instruction How to Play the Transverse Flute).

and the greatest eighteenth-century authority on keyboard style. His exhaustive and penetrating treatise *Versuch über die wahre Art das Clavier zu spielen* (Essay on the True Art of Keyboard Playing) is one of those rare books on music whose quality, as distinct from its significance, has stood the test of centuries. Issued in 1762, the book is directed specifically at harpsichord and clavichord players but clearly acknowledges the power in the wings. 'The more recent pianoforte,' Bach writes, 'when it is sturdy and well built, has many fine qualities, although its touch must be carefully worked out, a task which is not without its difficulties.' In the years between 1762 and his death in 1788, Bach himself worked out that touch and much else besides to become one of the few unarguable masters of the new instrument, and saw it transformed, partly through his own efforts as a composer, from an exotic upstart into the heir apparent of the great keyboard tradition to which he himself had been so favourably born. During his long service at the court of Frederick the Great (an accomplished musician and composer himself), he had had ample opportunity to study the piano and had witnessed dramatic improvements in the instruments supplied by Silbermann, of whose pianos the king possessed no fewer than 15 when Johann Sebastian Bach paid his now famous visit.

Bach was by no means alone in his reservations. It is a curious fact that although the piano had been invented very early in the century, and on principles which remained fundamentally unaltered for the next hundred years, its advantages over the harpsichord were slow to be realized, and it was the best part of half a century before the long dominance of the older instrument began significantly to crumble. The explanation lies neither with the inadequacy of the earliest pianos nor with the intellectual thickness of eighteenth-century Europeans, but with profound changes in society and in the musical reflections of those changes. Instrumental music in the Baroque era, and keyboard music in particular, had been dominated by polyphony and counterpoint, culminating in the fugues of J. S. Bach. This was music in which design, beauty of line and the expressive interaction of melodic strands were paramount. To a degree unknown in the music of the nineteenth century the notes were the music and the music was the notes. Personal expression, as it came to be understood in the Romantic era (mirroring the infinitely subtle contours of the human voice) played an all but negligible role. The performer's initiative resided almost entirely in the realms of rhythm, articulation and tempo. As in earlier times, such music was essentially the province of an educated aristocracy and the professional musicians who served them.

With the rise of a mercantile middle class in the eighteenth century, this learned, sophisticated, 'aristocratic' art increasingly fell by the wayside, as the long reign of polyphony gave way to the simpler textures of accompanied melody, known in the trade as 'homophony'. As the role of the individual in society grew in importance, the ideal of personal expression assumed an ever more central place in the musical firmament. The rigid, 'terraced' dynamics of the harpsichord, while adequate to the contrapuntal and socially stratified requirements of the Baroque, were incompatible with the new humanism. An instrument that could not 'sigh' was no fit vehicle for the expression of personal emotion. The clavichord could do this – indeed its subtleties of inflection surpass even those of the modern piano – but its tiny sound ruled it out for anything more than sensitive soliloquizing. Like the lordly harpsichord, its days were numbered. Both instruments hung on into the beginning of the nineteenth century, but by then the course of music had already left them way behind. That Beethoven's early sonatas were designated as suitable for either piano or harpsichord was no more than a commercial ploy on the part of his publishers. By 1810, the harpsichord was as good as dead.

CHAPTER 2

A Spreading of Wings

The day of the piano, as we have seen, was a long time dawning. More than 50 years passed between its invention and its first public airing – in Vienna, in 1763 – and even then it seems to have made little impression. It was not until 1768, in Dublin, that it was publicly unveiled as a solo instrument, at the hands of a Mr Henry Walsh. A fortnight later, on 2 June, it made its solo debut in England, but on this occasion it was played by Johann Christian Bach, one of the most popular and fashionable musicians in London, to which he had moved from his native Germany seven years earlier. Now, at last, time, place and circumstance combined to welcome it. In only a short time, the piano took its place as the most fashionable instrument in town.

Yet the instrument was still in its relative infancy and was hardly without its limitations. For many years, indeed, it was outshone in brilliance and volume by the harpsichord and could only hint at the tenderness and subtlety of the clavichord. Its tone was thin and brittle, and its mechanism noisy and notoriously unreliable. Why then did it now so rapidly succeed? To a remarkable degree, the explanation lies in simple snobbery. J. C. Bach was more than just esteemed. He enjoyed the favour of George III and had for some time been music master to the queen. It needed little more, then, than its appearance at this royally favoured concert for the piano to be seized upon as a badge of respectability and social standing.

J. C. Bach was among music's most likeable personalities. Born in 1735, he was the youngest son of the great Johann Sebastian (who fathered 20 children), and was in many ways the most independent-minded. While his early training was overseen by his father, it was his elder brother Carl Philipp Emanuel who put the finishing touches to his formal education, by the end of which he had become a keyboard player of outstanding quality. He travelled to Italy in 1754 where he studied composition with Padre Martini, perhaps the most famous teacher in Europe, and became a skilled and successful composer of Italian opera (though not without getting himself banned from the stage of Milan's San Carlo Theatre for his conduct with a young ballerina). In 1761 he left Italy for England, produced two operas there and rapidly became a favourite at the court. With his friend and compatriot Carl Friedrich Abel he pioneered the institution of the public concert, and dominated London's musical life for the best part of 20 years.

From the beginning of his career, Bach had been a shrewd and unapologetic businessman. As he said of Carl Philipp Emanuel, 'My brother lives to compose; I compose to live.' His music – the last sonata of Op. 5 being a very notable exception – is generally lightweight and unassuming, designed to charm rather than to challenge, but it is supremely professional, and where the keyboard is concerned he wrote quite idiomatically for the inflective properties of the piano. His Op. 13 Concertos may say on the title page that they are suitable 'for Harpsichord or Piano Forte', but the style of the keyboard writing shows no such ambivalence.

*   *   *

In his famous reference to England as 'a nation of shopkeepers', Napoleon might be conceded a point. Had he substituted 'businessmen' for 'shopkeepers', however, his aim would have been still more acute, though at some cost to the intended insult. Shopkeepers, after all, were little men, petty cogs in the industrial machine which was transforming the political map of Europe more irrevocably than Napoleon himself. Businessmen, on the other hand, were wielders of power, well on their way to inheriting the earth – and nowhere more so than in Britain. Whatever they may have lacked in culture and refinement, these were men with their heads screwed on straight, unsentimental realists who understood the market place and knew how to manipulate it. A nation of businessmen was no pushover. No one understood this better than Johannes Zumpe, a former apprentice to Silbermann and one of a dozen German instrument makers, known as 'The Twelve Apostles', who had emigrated to London in the wake of the Seven Years' War.

As a craftsman, Zumpe was not in the same league as his old master, but he was no charlatan either. His instruments were well made and pleasing to the eye. What set him apart from his rivals was not so much his art, however, as his outlook. The rapidly evolving keyboard market in London was dominated at that time by the firms of Shudi, Broadwood and Kirkman, whose instruments, in the

George, third Earl Cowper and the Gore family, *painted by Zoffany in 1775.*
The piano is probably a Zumpe.

venerable tradition of the continental craftsman, were made exclusively
for the moneyed aristocracy, and were priced accordingly. Zumpe was
the first to recognize the potential custom of the rising middle classes
and set out to make and market pianos at a price they could afford.
To that end, he simplified Cristofori's action, which had remained
essentially unaltered through five decades, and adopted the modest
rectangular form of the clavichord. His success was almost instan-
taneous and he rapidly entered the history books as 'the father of the
commercial piano'. While his instruments may not have compared in
quality with those of his rivals, they were simple to make, relatively
cheap to buy and quickly delivered (on the back of a solitary porter).
With Zumpe, to an extent unmatched by any of his colleagues or
predecessors, the craft of piano making became a business. Only

J. L. Dussek (1760–1812).

shortly after his arrival in London in 1760 he was making a fortune, which he retired to enjoy at an early age. Meanwhile, across the English Channel, the progress of the piano, and those who played it, was proceeding apace. Among the latter was a figure much admired in his time, but almost entirely forgotten by posterity until the late twentieth century, when he enjoyed at least a partial resurrection.

Born in Bohemia in 1760, four years after Mozart and 28 years after Haydn (who was in any case never more than a competent pianist), Jan Ladislav Dussek was one of the first touring virtuosos, and is said to have been the first pianist ever to play with his profile to the audience. With Clementi, he was one of the pioneers of the new 'singing' style of piano playing. His writing for the instrument is often brilliantly virtuosic and in many ways anticipates both the styles and the techniques of such later composers as Schubert, Beethoven, Weber, Mendelssohn, Rossini, Chopin and Schumann.

There can be no doubting that both J. C. Bach and Dussek were very considerable pianists, but it was Bach's young friend Mozart who was to become the first great one (they had met in London in 1764, when Mozart was eight and being carted around Europe as a child prodigy).* At the time of his birth in 1756, the piano's evolution on the European mainland lagged behind its development in Britain. The most obvious formative influences on Mozart's keyboard style were the harpsichord, the clavichord, and to a very much lesser extent, the

---

*Mozart, it should be noted, was the most brilliant but by no means the first child prodigy to be exhibited in London. Nor did his visit succeed in elevating the English taste for oddities in general. Memories of the Austrian *Wunderkind* did nothing to curb the ardour with which Londoners received a touring Italian with his chorus of 11 cats, nor did they diminish the rapture occasioned by a three-year-old master of the kettledrums.

organ. Less obvious, but more significant in the long run, was his almost equal familiarity with the violin and viola, both of them acutely inflective instruments (far removed from the angular, mechanistic juxtapositions of the harpsichord), and his intimate acquaintance with the human voice. The ideal of song permeates his music in almost every medium, complemented by the unerring dramatic instinct that made him the greatest opera composer who ever lived. The piano, with its capacity to imitate the rise and fall of human speech, was the perfect keyboard instrument for a composer whose musical personality was fundamentally grounded in the nature of dialogue. For the same reason, the classical concept of sonata form, with its alternating periods of stability and flux, and its principled opposition of contrasting groups or themes, might almost have been invented for him. More than any other keyboard instrument, the piano offered Mozart a variety of contrasts and a subtlety of inflection perfectly suited to his expressive and developmental cast of mind.

Inevitably, this determined his approach to the playing of it, which like his harmony in later years was quietly revolutionary. The standard practice of the day was to employ a relatively detached touch, giving notes, as a rule, rather less than their written value; yet Mozart's oft-expressed ideal of piano-playing was that it should 'flow like oil'. In his playing as in his music, he was the very essence of discretion: controlled, meticulously attentive to detail, translucent in texture, rhythmically supple yet metrically exact, and immaculate in execution. His recipe for ideal performance, as summarized in a letter to his sister, was a judicious blend of 'expression, taste and fire – but always with complete precision'. In his letters he places the greatest stress on beauty of tone, and was therefore probably rather restricted in his dynamic range, particularly at the upper end of the scale. He was likewise sparing in his use of the sustaining pedal, though his letters leave no doubt that he did use it, and regarded it as an important resource.

Mozart's greatest music, and his piano concertos in particular, may transport us to a kind of symbolic Utopia, in which opposing tensions are miraculously resolved, but he remained an eminently practical composer. Unlike Beethoven, who increasingly wrote for tomorrow, Mozart composed for the here and now. Apart from the intrinsic evidence of his music there is no more illuminating window on his pianistic ideals than a long letter to his family praising the instruments of the Augsburg builder Johann Andreas Stein.

Stein was himself an accomplished and sensitive musician, and through his legacy of more than 700 pianos, which were widely copied, he became the founding father of the Viennese tradition in piano building, though he himself remained and died in his native Bavaria. The most far-reaching of his many contributions was the invention of the so-called 'hopper action', whereby the hammer is enabled to fall away from the string while the activating key is still depressed (a mechanism generally referred to, for obvious reasons, as 'escapement'). In his acutely observant report, Mozart comments:

> Before I ever saw any of Stein's work, I liked Spaeth's pianos the best; but now I have to give Stein's preference, for they are much better than the Regensburg instruments. When I play vigorously, whether I leave the finger down or lift it up, the tone is finished the moment I sound it. I can attack the keys in any way I want, the tone will always be even, it will not block, will not come out too loud or too soft, or perhaps even fail to sound; in one word, everything is even. True, he will not let such a piano go for less than 300 florins, but the trouble he takes and the diligence he applies are beyond price. His instruments have this distinguishing feature: they are made with an escapement. Not one man in a hundred bothers with this; but without an escapement it is impossible for a pianoforte not to block or leave an aftersound. When you strike the keys, his hammers fall back again the instant they jump against the strings, whether you leave the keys down or up. When he has finished such an instrument (as he tells me), he first sits down and tries over all kinds of passages, runs and jumps, and whittles and works away so long until the piano does everything; for he works only for the benefit of the music and not for his own benefit alone, otherwise he would be finished right away. He says often, 'If I were not myself such a passionate lover of music and were not able to do a little bit myself on the piano, I would certainly have lost patience with my work long ago; however, I am a

lover of instruments that do not deceive the player, and which are durable.' And *his* pianos really *are* durable. He guarantees that the sounding-board will not break or crack. When he has a sounding-board ready, he sets it out in the air, rain, snow, heat of the sun and all hell, so that it cracks open; then he inserts wedges and glues them in, so that it becomes really strong and firm. He is quite glad when it cracks; you can be sure then that nothing more is going to happen to it. Quite often he even cuts into it himself and glues it together again and fixes it right ... I have played all my six sonatas* by heart quite often ... the last one, in D, comes out incomparably on Stein's pianos. The machine which you press with the knee is likewise better made on his instruments than on any others; I need scarcely touch it and it works, and as soon as I take away the knee the least bit, you don't hear the slightest aftersound.†

In old age, Stein's business was mainly carried on by his family, most particularly by his daughter Nanette, one of the most remarkable figures in the history of the piano. Herself a pianist of genius, according to Mozart's own report, she appeared in concert, as well as playing privately for Mozart and Beethoven (a close friend), and in 1794 married Johann Andreas Streicher, another exceptional figure: a lifelong friend of the poet Schiller, he achieved distinction as a composer, teacher and virtuoso pianist, as well as entering into the business with his wife. In 1816, Nanette built a piano for Beethoven boasting the then unusual compass of six and a half octaves. Alfred Dolge's claim that nearly all of Beethoven's compositions were created on pianos built by Nanette Streicher is, however, quite inaccurate.

* * *

While Mozart's greatness as composer and pianist is of course beyond doubt, he was not unchallenged – a fact confirmed by his part in history's first great pianistic combat. Musical 'duels' date back at least

---

* K279–84.

† Many music lovers have been puzzled by the apparent absence of pedals in photographs of some period instruments. In these, the raising and lowering of the dampers were effected, as Mozart indicates, by knee levers just below the casing.

as far as ancient Greece, and if we include the 'cutting contests' of the early jazz musicians, continued well into our own century. Of the many specifically pianistic duels, two stand out above all others: the battle of Mozart and Clementi in 1781 and that between Liszt and Thalberg in 1837 (see p. 68). Both were engineered by royalty, the first by Emperor Joseph II of Austria, who had bet the Grand Duchess that Mozart would prove himself superior to Clementi. The two celebrities arrived as bidden and were put through their paces, improvising, performing works of their own, sight-reading sonatas and then improvising together at two pianos on a theme taken from these works. The outcome was predictably inconclusive, but the Emperor was gracefully conceded to have won his wager, it being agreed, in a burst of courtly double-talk, that 'while Clementi had only art, Mozart had both art and taste'. Clementi was fulsome in his praise of Mozart, and as his subsequent compositions demonstrate, derived long-term benefits from the encounter. Mozart was characteristically nasty about Clementi, but thought highly enough of his Sonata in B flat, Op. 6, No. 2 (Clementi's contribution to the proceedings) to pinch one of its themes for his own *Magic Flute* overture. And though he was too ungenerous to admit it, his music suggests that he discovered new aspects of the piano and its usage from a man whose importance in pianistic history was in some ways greater than his own.

Variously described as 'The Columbus of the Piano', 'The Father of the Modern Piano School' and 'The Founder of Piano Technique', Muzio Clementi is remembered today almost exclusively by piano students, and by most of them for a single, tepid little Sonatina in C. Despite the concentrated efforts of no less a figure than Vladimir Horowitz, it seems unlikely that there will ever be a major revival of interest in his compositions.

He was born into a musical Italian family in 1752, four years before Mozart, whose damning judgment has blighted his reputation for well over two centuries. In 1766, now 14 and a brilliant performer on the harpsichord and organ, he was effectively purchased from his parents by a travelling English aristocrat who removed him to the wilds of

Dorset and undertook to oversee his education. In 1770 Clementi made a sensational London debut as a pianist, and soon came to be widely recognized as a major force on the European musical scene. More important than Clementi's compositions was his approach to the piano, in which he was very much tomorrow's man. As noted above, the earlier Classicists had cultivated a relatively detached touch at the keyboard (the treatises of the time leave no doubt that the vocal-style *legato*, that Mozartian 'flowing like oil' so beloved of the coming Romantics, was then the exception rather than the rule). Nor, on the whole, did they indulge in very great contrasts of volume. If Czerny is to be believed, Beethoven, two years before his death in 1827, recalled even Mozart's playing as

The title page of Clementi's Gradus ad Parnassum, *1817.*

being 'neat and clean, but rather flat and antiquated'. Clementi was the first really influential pianist who openly rejected these conventions, pursuing a more wide-ranging, heroic, dramatically poetic ideal. The fact is that it was Clementi, not Mozart, who had the most formative influence on Beethoven's playing, and on his vision of the instrument.

In his concentration on fast thirds, sixths and octaves, his gladiatorial recourse to bravura, his thundering chords and arpeggios and his unprecedented stamina, Clementi paved the way as well for Liszt, Brahms, even Ravel (just as the Mozartian line of descent, with its emphasis on finesse of line, translucency of texture and harmonic 'light', runs from Hummel through Mendelssohn and Chopin to Debussy). His epoch-making book of studies, *Gradus ad Parnassum* (1817), was the first of its kind and is still in use today. In his teaching,

Clementi shaped a generation. Among his many distinguished pupils were Field, Cramer (much admired by Beethoven), Moscheles and Meyerbeer. Nor did his influence stop there. He became in turn a music publisher and a prosperous piano manufacturer, and ended his days as a wealthy English squire.

That Clementi as a manufacturer should have achieved such success over so many years is in itself a tribute to the quality of the instruments his company produced. In the late eighteenth and early nineteenth centuries, London was a hive of piano-building activity without equal in the world, and among its leading lights was a company still in business to this day.

The London firm of John Broadwood & Sons is the oldest piano manufacturer in existence. Founded in 1728 by the Swiss-born harpsi-chord maker Burkhard Tschudi, later 'anglicized' to Burkat Shudi, it passed on Shudi's death into the hands of the Scots-born John Broadwood (his son-in-law and partner from 1769 and 1770 respec-tively) on Shudi's death in 1773. In that year, the firm's first pianos appeared, although in truth there was little to distinguish them from Zumpe's save the name. It wasn't until seven years later that Broad-wood produced a piano of his own design. From then on, many of his innovations, like those of his sons and further descendants, were widely adopted, in some cases near universally.

Before considering their nature and significance, however, it might be useful to take stock of the industry as a whole at around this time, and to review the character and design of its major products.

At the end of the eighteenth century, three basic designs were in common use: that of the 'grand', as we call it today, which retained the essential, wing-shaped structure of the harpsichord (many of its structural requirements and principles being the same); the upright – still very much with us, of course; and the so-called 'Square', whose rectangular, box-like form (it was never literally square at all) grew out of the fad for reconstructed clavichords. Indeed in form and general construction they were little different from their pre-decessors, save for the metal strings, a considerably strengthened

A square piano made in London by J. C. Zumpe, 1767.

frame, necessitated by the resulting increase in tension, and of course the hammer action.

The first known square piano was built in Germany in 1742 by Johann Socher, almost twenty years before Zumpe produced the first English model. Having more or less cornered the market for several years, Zumpe was later overtaken by John Broadwood, whose first 'original' square pianos date from 1780, and whose clients were to include some of the greatest musicians of their day, Beethoven foremost amongst them. By 1775 Johann Behrend had exhibited his square piano in Philadelphia, and within a year of that event Sébastien Erard in Paris produced the first French model, so close in design to Broadwood's that it bordered on grand larceny, but Broadwood was not in a position to complain. Despite its evident success in marketing terms, the instrument even now left a good deal to be desired. Its tone, in particular, was weak and rasping and was hardly to be compared with that of the grand. In the early 1780s, however, Broadwood hit on the idea of moving the wrest plank* from the right-hand side (its

---

*That part of a keyboard instrument into which the tuning-pins are driven.

traditional siting in the clavichord) to the back of the case. The improvement in tone and volume exceeded his best hopes and transformed the construction of square pianos from that day forward. Within a short time it was universally adopted, and with it, strange to say, the European contribution to the instrument's evolution came unexpectedly to a halt. Thereafter, all significant improvements came from America, where the square piano enjoyed a unique popularity for the best part of a century. A noteworthy feature of Broadwood's patent of 1783 was the inclusion of pedals for raising the dampers and shifting the action sideways (the so-called 'sustaining' pedal, frequently miscalled the 'loud' pedal, since by raising all the dampers it allows the sympathetic vibration of unstruck strings throughout the piano's compass, and the *una corda* or 'soft' pedal, which originally restricted the hammer to only one of the strings allotted to each note).

The staying power of the upright piano is a matter of record. And wherever space is at a premium its virtues speak for themselves. Among its earliest pioneers was Christian Friederici, whose first models date from the 1730s, but even then the idea was hardly new. As early as 1480, the harpsichord had been up-ended, with its action suitably adapted, and was given the grandiloquent name of 'Clavicytherium'. In 1795 William Stodart of London applied the same idea to the grand piano, and three years later William Southwell of Dublin tried the same thing with a square piano. In each of these cases, however, the instrument rested on a stand. Not until 1800 did it occur to anyone to dispense with this and let the instrument rest upon the floor, and then, as happens so often in the history of inventions, it occurred to two men simultaneously, on opposite sides of the Atlantic: Matthias Müller in Vienna and Isaac Hawkins in Philadelphia. Not to be verbally upstaged by the ghost of the Clavicytherium, Müller dubbed his invention the 'Ditanaklasis'. The gloves were off. Pleyel et Cie of Paris responded with their 'Harmomelo'. Southwell, further modifying his upturned square of 1798, was having none of this pretentious continental pseudo-Greco claptrap. He marketed his latest model in 1811 under the descriptive but hardly seductive title of 'Piano Sloping Backwards'.

By whatever name, the upright piano was here to stay.

Clementi in England and Streicher in Vienna were by no means the only pianists turned piano manufacturers. By the middle of the nineteenth century there were a goodly number, of whom more anon. Among the earliest and most illustrious was the Parisian firm of Pleyel et Cie, established in partnership with the pianist–composer Friedrich Kalkbrenner in 1807. Pleyel was himself a noted pianist and composer and had had the honour of studying composition with Haydn, no less.

In 1792, the year after Mozart's death at 35, a pianistic bombshell burst over the Viennese musical scene. The detonator was a squat, swarthy, uningratiating young man of 22. Born in the provincial city of Bonn in Germany, he was to

Clavicytherium, with doors opened.

change the face of Western music to a degree unmatched by any musician before or since. Even as a youth, he fairly bristled with arrogance. Later, when he was famous, he declared, 'I acknowledge only one morality, and that is the morality of power.'

Power he had, with a vengeance. As a pianist, Ludwig van Beethoven was the first to overwhelm the instrument with the force of his own personality. Compared to Mozart or Clementi, his playing may have been a trifle rough and elemental. In his playing as in his music, Mozart had been content, generally speaking, to work within the confines of eighteenth-century manners and eighteenth-century instruments. He too was a revolutionary in his way, but he worked by stealth. He was a subversive rather than a guerrilla. Beethoven, on the other hand, was a born iconoclast, prepared to rock any boat, wring any withers, and to challenge all comers. He was the first pianist regularly to overpower his audiences, drawing them into a world of emotional intensity and spiritual daring the like of which had never been experienced before. Particularly in his incomparable improvisations, he often moved his listeners not merely to tears but to uncontrollable sobbing. He tore aside the curtains of eighteenth-century reserve and laid bare the realities of life with a courage bordering on ruthlessness. Even before his Viennese debut, critics recognized the sheer danger in Beethoven's playing. As Carl Junker observed in 1791, 'His playing differs greatly from the usual method of treating the piano. It seems as if he has struck out on an entirely new path for himself.' As indeed he had. No one was more acutely aware of this than Beethoven himself. Whatever he may have lacked in the way of social graces, he more than made up for in self-confidence. Indeed it was a part of his attraction.

As early as the middle 1790s Anton Reicha recalled turning pages for Beethoven in a concerto: 'I was mostly occupied in wrenching the strings of the piano which snapped, while the hammers stuck among the broken strings ... Back and forth I leaped, jerking out a string, disentangling a hammer, turning a page – I worked harder than Beethoven.' Nor was the composer's frustration confined to matters

Upright piano (1801) by Isaac Hawkins of Philadelphia.

of volume. He chafed under the restrictions of the piano's range. The standard grand of the early 1800s had a compass of only five and a half octaves (as against the seven-plus we take for granted today). It was a great day for Beethoven when Broadwood of London sent him in 1818 a magnificent instrument with a compass of six and a half octaves and a reservoir of power then unknown in Viennese instruments. Never had an instrument of such grandeur been accorded a more royal progress. Departing from the London docks, it was shipped to

Trieste by way of Gibraltar before being carried by horse-drawn cart over unpaved mountain tracks for more than 300 miles on its way to the Austrian capital. And though he soon reduced it to a ruin, 'its strings broken and tangled, like a thorn bush whipped by a storm' (Johann Stumpff), 'its innards blackened by overturned inkwells' (Ferdinand Ries), and its upper registers mute – 'as dumb as the musician himself was deaf' (Sir John Russell) – it inspired him to some of his greatest achievements. Indeed it received its musical baptism with the low C which ends the first movement of his last sonata, Op. 111.

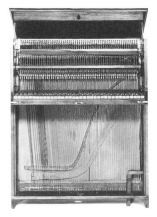

Interior of a Hawkins upright piano (1801).

Like Mozart and Clementi before him, Beethoven was not averse to a little pianistic duelling, although in his case there was no ambiguity about the results. Those colleagues who accepted the challenge quickly lived to regret it, but none of them was in the Clementi class. On the other hand, Joseph Gelinek, a piano-playing priest, had been warmly praised by Mozart. Not so the melodramatic Daniel Steibelt, famed for his shivering *tremolandos* (a man before his time, he would have found his true niche in the silent cinema). This curious gentleman, whose concerts were often accompanied by his wife on the tambourine, was probably 80 per cent charlatan, but there is enough contemporary evidence to suggest that the remaining 20 per cent may well have been authentic genius, if of a relatively minor kind.

If Beethoven had no serious rival as a pianist, the same, surprisingly, could not be said of Beethoven the composer. However odd it may seem today, there was one man whose piano sonatas, though numbering only four, were held by a substantial body of connoisseurs to be at least equal if not indeed superior to Beethoven's.

Between 1810 and 1820 the most radical and far-reaching ideas about the piano, both writing for it and playing on it, came from a

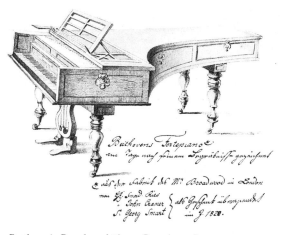

Beethoven's Broadwood piano. Drawing, 1827.

man who seldom if ever performed in public. An ex-prodigy, Carl Maria von Weber was a keyboard virtuoso on a par with the greatest of his day. But while figures like Moscheles or Hummel (of whom more anon) belonged to the elegant, classically oriented school of pianism pioneered by J. C. Bach and Mozart, Weber belonged to that parallel line of descent originating with C. P. E. Bach and Clementi. In Weber, it might be argued, we encounter the first of the great Romantics. His keyboard music was orchestral in scope but supremely pianistic in style, peppered with dare-devil leaps, coruscating passage-work and stretches which memorialize two of the biggest hands in the business (he could reach a twelfth in both hands, which even allowing for the narrower keys of the day, was almost freakish). In the A flat Sonata, for instance, the left hand is called upon to play a solid, unrolled chord comprising (in ascending order) A♭–E♭–A♭–C. The teenage Liszt, already an incomparable virtuoso, is said to have declared that Weber's music was to other music 'as the gigantic nature of the New World and the virgin forests of America are to the belted, box-treed, enclosed gardens of Europe'. In the nineteenth century there was hardly a pianist to be found whose repertoire did not include

Carl Maria von Weber (1786–1826). Portrait (1825) by Ferdinand Schimon.

the A flat Sonata, the famous *Invitation to the Dance*, the *Polacca brillante* and the still splendidly effective Konzertstück in F minor for piano and orchestra, all of which have survived the test of time.

Of comparable importance in his time was another composer–virtuoso whose works and whose playing were frequently likened to Beethoven's. Johann Nepomuk Hummel (1778–1837), a pupil of Mozart and Haydn, was among the most important figures in the transition from the Classical to the Romantic era, and had a formative influence on the young Chopin, whose piano concertos owe a direct debt to his own. Like both Beethoven and Chopin, he was an improviser of genius and a pianist, according to Czerny, of unrivalled clarity and elegance (and, it would seem, ostentation: he dressed in the most vulgar fashion and wore diamond rings on almost every finger). Like his elder colleague Dussek, he paid a heavy price for his success. So expansive was his girth in later years that a space had to be cut out of his dining-room table to render the condiments accessible to his reach.

In 1827, on a trip to Vienna to visit the dying Beethoven, Hummel was introduced to a young musician, 30 years of age and a native of the city, whose name – Franz Schubert – was entirely new to him. They enjoyed a short but mutually cordial acquaintance and Schubert dedicated his last three piano sonatas to Hummel, though both men were dead by the time they were published. Schubert was a fluent and infinitely subtle pianist, but like Haydn he was never a virtuoso. Nor, on the whole, did he write virtuoso music, though much of it is far from easy. Like Tchaikovsky and Ravel, he sometimes wrote beyond his own capacities as a performer – indeed he was probably the first great com-

Johann Nepomuk Hummel (1778–1837). Engraving by Senefelder.

poser to do so. Halfway through the great fugue in his Lisztian *Wanderer Fantasy* (a work, characteristically, with a song at its heart),* he once threw up his hands in defeat, crying, 'Let the devil play this! *I* can't!'

While his great sonatas languished all but unknown for a hundred years (in 1927, the centenary of Schubert's death, no less a figure than Rachmaninov was unaware of their existence), his smaller pieces – the two sets of Impromptus, the six *Moments Musicaux*, a cornucopia of waltzes, Ländler and Écossaises, and a host of songs – were among the best-sellers of the nineteenth century (a tragic irony, in view of his death in poverty and obscurity at the age of 31). Like most of the great composer–pianists, Schubert was a marvellously inventive improviser, and his hundreds of dances for the piano probably give a reliable impression of the music that used to tumble out of his imagination whenever he sat at a keyboard. Not that he required a piano: legend has it that he began writing his superlative Octet on the tablecloth of a Viennese café.

With Schubert's death in 1828 (the year after Beethoven's), the first great chapter in the life of the piano came to an end. The Classical era, which had put a premium on balance, symmetry of form, clarity of outline and closely reasoned development, had survived the French Revolution, the First Empire and the Napoleonic Wars. The piano almost hadn't. Yet in the decades to come it was to emerge as the most significant, the most successful, the most symbolically potent instrument ever made.

---

*Schubert's own song *Der Wanderer*, D493, provides the basis of the work's slow movement.

CHAPTER 3

The Birth of a Style

Composers were not long in adapting the style of their music to the unique properties of the new instrument. The highly ornamented prolongations of the Baroque gave way increasingly to a simpler form of lyric melody, as the model of the human voice moved ever closer to the centre of musical aesthetics. The music tells its own story, tracing a consistent line of development through the works of C. P. E. and J. C. Bach, C. P. E.'s pupil Dussek, and onwards to the mature keyboard works of Mozart, Haydn, Clementi, Hummel, Beethoven and Schubert, all of whom wrote expressly for the piano and cultivated a broadly arching, *cantabile* style of melody.

Few musical journeys are more fascinating or illuminating than the careful perusal of C. P. E. Bach's keyboard music. Here, before our eyes and ears, the rise of the piano and the fall of the harpsichord are played out in a series of tableaux as rich in character as they are in significance. It was not for their significance, however, but for their art and emotional power that they were deeply admired by Mozart, Clementi and Beethoven, among many others. 'He is the father,' said Mozart, 'and we the children.' Clementi went even further. 'Whatever I understand of the pianoforte,' he wrote, 'I learned from his book.'*

Bach's invaluable treatise deals comprehensively with every aspect of keyboard technique and interpretation and was the pre-eminent authority on the subject for more than 6o years. Among many other areas in which it remains a vital source is its treatment of embellishments (turns, trills, the decorative and structural use of auxiliary notes, etc.), and more importantly, of their underlying purpose. One paragraph in particular should be taken to heart by 98 per

---

* *Versuch über die wahre Art das Clavier zu spielen* (Essay on the True Art of Keyboard Playing).

cent of pianists currently before the public, whose treatment of sonata forms and all similarly circular structures regularly fails to deal adequately with their reliance on repetition.* In music, and this may be particularly true of the Classical era (say, 1770–1830), it can hardly be stressed too strongly that context alters content, that 'mere' repetition is – or should be – so rare as to be positively exotic. Thus C. P. E. Bach's observations are applicable far beyond the narrow confines of embellishment:

> Variation when passages are repeated is indispensable today. It is expected of every performer. The public demands that practically every idea be repeatedly altered, sometimes without investigating whether the structure of the piece or the skill of the performer permits such alteration. It is this embellishing alone, especially if it is coupled with a long and sometimes bizarrely ornamented cadenza, that often squeezes the *Bravos* out of most listeners. But how lamentably are those two adornments of performance misused!

Squeezing *bravos* out of listeners is an important function of performers, and this was not an aspect of his youngest brother's education that C. P. E. Bach would have overlooked. Indeed the ability to wring cheers from his audience was among the many charms of Johann Christian Bach without which he could never have dominated the concert life of London for so long. For such an accomplished and popular player, however, he wrote surprisingly little for keyboard alone. His main contributions to the repertoire are two sets of six sonatas, Op. 5 (1767) and Op. 17, published posthumously.

---

*The basic form of the Classical sonata movement is a three-part, symmetrical structure in which the third part is thematically a repetition of the first: A (exposition), B (development), A¹ (recapitulation). The middle is a more fluid, improvisational mix, generally based on themes from the opening exposition. As the exposition is customarily repeated before proceeding to the central development section, this means that we hear its basic material three times over (although the opposition of contrasting keys, which is a vital feature of the exposition, is homogenized in the recapitulation).

The first of these had been seen in manuscript by the eight-year-old Mozart on his visit to London. Mozart spoke of Bach throughout his life with affection and admiration, and paid double tribute to their friendship – embracing an age gap of 21 years – first by arranging some of these sonatas as concerto movements (this while he was still a child), later by basing the slow movement of his beautiful A major Piano Concerto, K414, on a theme of Bach's.

Both sets of sonatas are well worth exploring: not masterpieces, maybe, but unworthy of neglect. The first sonata of all is both the weakest musically and the most revealing sociologically. Undemanding in every way, it amounts to little more than bait on the hook, ensnaring the attention of well-heeled young ladies whose minds and fingers were as yet unequal to the more substantial fare concealed within.

There is a curious irony in the fact that the first genuinely great piano composer to have held his place in the mainstream repertoire was not himself a virtuoso at all. Indeed we know next to nothing about Joseph Haydn as a pianist, yet his 62 piano sonatas are not only vastly more numerous but traverse a far richer and more varied terrain than either Mozart's or Clementi's. Their variety alone is often as striking as in Beethoven, and the range of his keyboard styles is comparably wide, from simple song-like structures, whose unimaginative bass lines sometimes border on banality, to massive, quasi-orchestral sonorities (as in the magnificent E flat Sonata that crowns the series) and sinuous rhythms of wonderful complexity.

It used to be thought that most of Haydn's keyboard works were conceived for the harpsichord, but this is likely to be true only of the first 19, many of which recall Scarlatti at his most cosy and domestic. From 1767 onwards, it now seems safe to assume, all of Haydn's solo sonatas were written expressly for the piano, and in certain cases there are pedal markings to prove it (one in the great C major, No. 60 in the H. C. Robbins Landon catalogue, seems almost to anticipate the Beethoven of the 'Moonlight' and 'Waldstein' Sonatas). More prophetic still is the range of Haydn's compass here, going up to a top A fully a decade before Beethoven did likewise (again in the 'Waldstein',

Joseph Haydn (1732–1809), painted by Thomas Hardy on a visit to London in 1792.

also in C major). Certainly the scale of his thinking and the scope of his instrumental imagination expands dramatically at about this time – it can hardly be that he had belatedly discovered a host of hitherto unsuspected resources in the harpsichord. On the whole, his approach to keyboard textures is more rugged than Mozart's, dealing in more substantial blocks of sound, often favouring harmonic colouring and rhythmic momentum over the ultra-refined, vocal-style melodies so common in Mozart. Both he and Mozart freely acknowledged their debt to C. P. E. Bach, as we have seen, but it is in Haydn's sonatas, for all their originality, that the line of succession is more easily heard.

The D major Sonata (L50) from 1780 [CD 1] is one of the few to have achieved real popularity with amateurs and professionals alike, and no wonder. In its festive high spirits, its Handelian echoes and its relative brevity it makes for a very agreeable 11 minutes or so. For all its ceremonial air, the first movement is of modest proportions, and its brief central development section, drawing on both main themes, is characteristically ingenious and moving, introducing just enough harmonic fluidity to make the return to stability in the exposition a real event. The Largo is expressive out of all proportion to its brevity, and the playful, wide-ranging Finale makes a delicious contrast to the ceremonial demeanour and strumming, drum-like repetitions of the first movement.

*   *   *

For reasons never satisfactorily explained, Mozart's output for solo piano seldom even hints at the quality of his concertos or his chamber music with piano, nor does the problem have anything to do with instrumentation: the great Sonata for two Pianos, for example, *is* of comparable quality, as are the last two of his sonatas for piano duet. Yet of the solo works, only a handful can be mentioned in the same breath as his symphonies, concertos, operas and chamber music, and of these perhaps only three can be found among his 17 solo sonatas (those in A minor and C minor, and the late D major, K576). When it comes to such one-offs as the great B minor Adagio, K540, and the

Mozart's birthplace and family home (1747–73) in the Getreidegasse, Salzburg: interior view. The piano was built by Anton Walter of Vienna in 1780 and bought by Mozart in 1784.

extraordinary, pungently chromatic Minuet in D, K355, there we are unquestionably in the presence of a great composer composing greatly. More significant than either, however, is the haunting A minor Rondo, K511 [CD 1].

The most lavishly and revealingly marked of all Mozart's piano works, this infinitely subtle piece grants us a unique insight into the probable character of his own playing. The idiom is perfectly attuned to the nature of the new instrument. This is a work whose performance on the harpsichord would be unthinkable, yet there is never the slightest striving after effect. Its suppleness of line and deftly applied shadings are of extraordinary naturalness. In its combination of eloquence and restraint, it seems to look forward to Chopin (just as Chopin so often looks back at Mozart). The closest parallel with Chopin, however, is to be found in a passage where Mozart comes as close as notationally possible to demonstrating his approach to *rubato*, an approach identical to that enunciated quite independently by Chopin almost half a century later – namely that deviations from strict tempo should be confined to the right-hand melody, the left hand holding unwaveringly to the metrical pulse.

In his letters, Mozart places the greatest stress on beauty of tone, and his playing (again like Chopin) was probably rather restricted in its dynamic range, particularly at the upper end of the scale, yet the use and variety of his accentuations are both subtle and vigorous. There is nothing effete about this music. At the same time, Mozart the musician was a perfect gentleman, not a rocker of boats. In his piano music there is never the slightest sense of strain, nor any whiff of frustration. Unlike Beethoven, Clementi, Liszt and Chopin, he cannot really be said to have pushed forward the frontiers of piano music or piano making. What he did was to set a new standard for the truly idiomatic use of the instrument as it had then evolved, bringing an aristocratic grandeur and an unsurpassed subtlety to the music written for and played on it.

Engraving of Muzio Clementi (1752–1832).

This has not, however, prevented commentators given to simplistic pronouncements from proclaiming that 'the first piece of music entirely suitable to the pianoforte' was in fact the Sonata in C major, Op. 2, No. 2 by Clementi (published in 1779, dedicated to Haydn and much admired by C. P. E. Bach). That it is entirely suited to the piano is perfectly true, as are all of Clementi's sonatas, but its virtuoso character, combined with Mozart's contemptuous dismissal of Clementi as a charlatan, has contributed to a misleading picture of the composer as a shallow, bravura technician, interested only in effect. The remarkable F sharp minor Sonata of 1785 [CD 1] is an eloquent corrective to this view. Searching and reflective, and with unexpected echoes of Scarlatti, its three movements are all in the minor key, and while undeniably pianistic they bear not a trace of the meretricious *mechanicus* suggested by Mozart.

Mozart, Clementi and Haydn all wrote idiomatically for the piano, yet strange to say, it was not until the Nocturnes of Clementi's pupil John Field (1782–1837) that anyone grasped the full importance and almost limitless potential of the sustaining pedal – the clearest of all bequests from Hebenstreit's harmonically sonorous pantaleon. Field's widely spaced, rolling, arpeggiated accompaniments were the first to exploit the unique harmonic and colouristic possibilities of the instrument and had a demonstrable effect on such far greater composers as Chopin, Mendelssohn and Liszt. Unfortunately, in the view of one writer at least, the melodies which they so luxuriantly support tend to be of mind-numbing insipidity.

This was never the case with Schubert. If Mozart's is the piano music of a largely Italianate opera composer, and Beethoven's that of a symphonist, Schubert's is self-evidently the work of an incomparable songwriter. Standing midway between Mozart and Liszt, and with more than a sideways nod to Beethoven, much of it set the tone for that sea of miniatures and self-contained character pieces that all but engulfed the domestic piano throughout the nineteenth century. Most of it was never conceived for the concert hall.

Despite his fluency at the keyboard, Schubert was not a composer like Chopin, who seemed to think through his fingers. Schubert's musical impulses often paid scant heed to the practical realities of piano technique. There are numerous passages in his sonatas, for instance, which are actually harder to master than many a flashier, saloniste showpiece. Yet the music, for the most part, is compounded of grace, subtlety, refinement and elegance, even when plumbing the depths of sorrow, as in the slow movement of his last sonata – the great B flat, D960. Schubert's piano music requires the greatest

A musical evening with Franz Schubert and his friends. The composer is at the piano with the singer J. M. Vogl. Oil sketch (1868) by Moritz von Schwind.

suppleness of line to sustain his broad, arching melodies, and the keenest ear for the iridescent harmonies that support and often transform them. Of equal importance, however, is the sheer toughness, the almost demoniacal drama that is also a part of his music. Nowhere, perhaps, is this more searingly evident than in his great setting of Goethe's poem *Erlkönig* (The Erl King) [CD 1] whose fiendish repeated octaves in the piano part depict the clattering hooves of a galloping horse as a man and his dying child attempt to outrun death. With this song the piano was promoted to a level of prominence and virtuosity that had no precedent in the form. Nor was this any mere fluke. In all of Schubert's greatest songs, and many less great, the piano is at the very least an equal partner.

Oddly enough, Beethoven, perhaps the most universal of all composers, was not, in the opinion of many professional singers, a great songwriter. The essence of his pianistic output is to be found in his unparalleled collection of 32 sonatas, which trace his emotional, stylistic and instrumental development from the blazing self-confidence of his 'angry young man' phase, through the crisis of his middle years, when the onset of deafness had him hovering on the brink of madness, to the transcendent spiritual and pianistic odyssey of his last six sonatas and the towering 'Diabelli' Variations. Hardly less remarkable, though, are the five mature concertos, the nine trios, the ten violin sonatas, the five cello sonatas and a host of lesser pieces. What gives this music its unique importance is the unequalled scope of its spiritual journeyings, the unpitying intellect controlling its expression, and the sheer genius and boldness of its formal daring. In its very universality, Beethoven's music posed a challenge to his successors which few were equipped to address.

Beethoven's final sonata, Op. 111, widely felt to be the greatest piano sonata ever written, is perhaps the most comprehensive self-portrait ever entrusted to the keyboard [CD 1]. Here, to a degree unmatched in any other work, we find Beethoven the titanic struggler with Fate (the turbulent, highly disciplined first movement, which uses every resource available in the piano of his time) and Beethoven the transcendental mystic (second movement), whose journey through the extremes of pain and despair resulted in music whose purity, serenity and awe are beyond the power of words to describe. Formally a theme and variations, this vale-dictory movement amounts by general con-sent to the most profound amen in pianistic history.

Beethoven's workroom in Vienna, drawn threee days after his death in 1827.

In purely instrumental terms, Beethoven expanded the tonal palette of the piano into realms scarcely hinted at before. His late sonatas are as supremely idiomatic as anything by Liszt, Chopin or Debussy, all of whom he prefigures in one way or another (not least in the mystical haze of his pedal markings in such works as the so-called 'Moonlight', 'Tempest' and 'Waldstein' sonatas). At the same time he seems frequently to have envisaged the piano as a kind of surrogate orchestra. Certainly no pianist, no composer, had ever made such revolutionary demands of the instrument before. As early as 1796 we find him writing to the piano maker Johann Streicher:

> There is no doubt that as far as the manner of playing it is concerned, the pianoforte is still the least studied and least developed of all instruments: often one thinks one is merely listening to a harp ... I hope the time will soon come when these two will be treated as entirely different instruments.

Even before the trail-blazingly dramatic 'Pathétique' Sonata of 1799 Beethoven was stretching the piano's capabilities. In the 'Appassionata'

A romantic image of Beethoven at the piano. Pastel, 19th century.

of 1805 he broke all records, and not a few strings. With his explosive accents, his chordal leaps and pounces, and his unprecedented dynamic range he revealed his impatience with instruments long before the late quartets and his famous outburst at the violinist Schuppanzigh: 'What do I care for your miserable fiddle when the spirit moves me?'

But the manufacturers had other things on their minds than the lofty visions of genius. If the piano was to survive, it would have to satisfy another, more numerous clientele.

CHAPTER 4

The Pride of the Parlour

Whatever the role of the performer in popularizing the piano, it was not in the concert hall but in the home that the instrument scored its greatest and most prolonged success. From Zumpe onwards, it was the domestic market more than any other that occupied the makers' minds. And the cannier of them realized early on that they had not merely to meet a demand but to create it. The purely musical attributes of their instruments were in many ways of secondary importance. The first priorities were practical and spatial. Southwell's 'Piano Sloping Backwards' of 1811 [see Chapter 2] may have been inelegantly named, but it represented a serious attempt at solving one of the three most intractable problems posed by all of the early uprights: while unarguably occupying less floor space than a grand, their inordinate height (in some cases exceeding nine feet) made them undesirable as furniture and alarmingly top-heavy. Performers were obliged to sit with their backs to the audience; and self-accompanying singers, of whom there were then many, had to sing away from rather than towards their listeners. But there were less high-minded motives for minimizing the size of the instrument.

A composite giraffe piano, possibly by C.C.E. van der Does, Amsterdam, 19th century.

With the fad for the piano firmly in the ascendant, manufacturers were keenly aware that, to paraphrase the great twentieth-century architect Mies van der Rohe, less was more. The smaller the piano, the more modest the rooms it could occupy, with a corresponding expansion of the potential market. By the simple expedient of lowering the body to just above floor level, Hawkins of Philadelphia reduced the height of his uprights to a mere four feet seven inches, despite the fact that the long bass strings still ran vertically from bottom to top on the left-hand side, exactly as in Stodart's up-ended grand of 1795. To render their appearance more symmetrical, these 'upright grands' were often encased in a stately rectangular box and very profitably marketed as 'cabinet' pianos, suitably decked out with 'radiated silk' frontages and carved, wooden cornices magni-

A W. W. Stodart cabinet piano of 1801, with doors closed and open.

loquently supported by 'pillars superior'. This was all well and good for the more affluent end of the middle-class market, with its pretentious aspirations, but more drastic action was required for their poorer and more humbly housed 'inferiors'.

In order to shrink the instrument still further without utterly destroying its character it was necessary to accommodate the same number and length of strings within a smaller compass. The pleasingly named Thomas Loud had experimented in 1802 with stretching the long bass strings diagonally, from the lower left to the upper right of the instrument, but it was his fellow Briton Robert Wornum who turned up trumps with his 'cottage' piano in 1813. At an average height of less than four feet, it could be accommodated by practically every parlour in the Western world. For rooms too small even for an upright, the early nineteenth-century shopper could purchase a small triangular piano, purpose-built to fit snugly in the corner. The most optimistic tribute to the equation of the piano with domesticity, however, must surely have been paid by an enterprising American architect who designed a block of flats for New York's Harlem with an upright piano built into the walls of every one.

Like the rest of its venerable family, the piano has always lived a double life: as a musical instrument on the one hand, and as an item of furniture on the other, in which capacity it has ineluctably been enshrined as a status symbol, a badge of respectability, an emblem of affluence. To this end, hardly less care and ingenuity have been devoted to its casing than to its mechanism. From its very earliest days, sculptors and painters have lavished nymphs, shepherds, wood sprites, serpents, dolphins and many other figures on its legs and sides. Alessandro Trasunti and other Italian makers went so far as to make detachable casings which could thus ennoble successive instruments of steadily improving quality.

Fallboards and music desks were frequently inlaid with gold and ivory, lids were decorated on both sides by exquisite paintings, including some by the greatest masters of the day, the pedals were supported by putti and dolphins – the sky, almost literally, was the

An Erard grand piano (c. 1840); marquetry case by George Henry Blake.

limit.* Among the items on display at the Great Exhibition of 1851 were John Champion Jones's 'Double or Twin Semi-Cottage Piano', featuring 'two fronts and sets of keys, one on either side, suitable for any number of players from one to six', and William Jenkins's 'Expanding and Collapsing Piano for Gentlemen's Yachts, the saloons of steam ships, ladies' cabins etc., only 13½ inches from front to back when collapsed'. At around the same time, Broadwood offered the potential buyer a mind-spinning choice of styles, including 'Sheraton, Jacobean, Tudor, Gothic, Louis XIII, XIV, XV and XVI, Flemish Renaissance, Elizabethan *cinquecento*, Queen Anne, Empire and Moorish'. The ingenious Pape of Paris, one of the most fertile designers in the history of the piano, could provide you with instruments of almost any size and shape: round, oval, hexagonal, pyramidic, concealed within a table or a writing desk, or brazenly displayed as a trendy conversation piece.

Eccentric approaches to the piano's appearance, however, were nothing new – witness some of the earliest uprights of Christian Friederici. One, dating from 1745, abandons the wing-shaped casing, determined by the respective lengths of the strings inside, in favour of an equilateral triangle – a procedure requiring a diagonal rather than a perpendicular stretching of the strings. Still more challenging to the

---

*In 1937, the German maker Blüthner encased a piano entirely in leather for its lofty but brief career aboard the ill-fated *Hindenburg* airship.

John Champion Jones's 'Twin Semi-Cottage Piano', c.1850.

builder's ingenuity, however, is a later model in which the strings, while arranged perpendicularly, are deployed so that the longest, lowest sounding ones were in the middle, and the shortest, highest sounding ones at either end. This freakish layout meant that keys on the extreme right controlled strings on the extreme left, and vice versa, hence their elaborate connection to long metal rods, activating hammers which could be as much as two feet away. There is perhaps no more tortuous a demonstration of the musical sacrifices made on the altar of an instrument's appearance.

The last third of the eighteenth century saw a great upsurge of interest in furniture and other items which behind a graceful exterior fulfilled a dual purpose. Thus we find as examples of the so-called 'harlequin' style, stepladders concealed in library tables, dressing tables disgorging camouflaged washstands, mirrors resplendently concealing dressing cases (and in some cases, even pianos). The concept of the dual-purpose piano reached its apex, however, with a patent filed in London in 1866 by a certain Mr Milward, who described it thus:

> The piano, in place of being supported by legs in the ordinary manner, is supported by a frame which again rests upon a hollow base; inside such hollow base is placed a couch, which is mounted upon rollers and can be drawn out in front of the piano ... A hollow space is formed in the middle of the frame for rendering the pedals accessible to the performer's feet, and on one side of such a space is formed a closet, having doors opening in front of the piano, and which is designed to contain the bedclothes. On the side of the space so formed, firstly, a

Graf 'Pyramid' piano, 1829.

bureau with drawers, and secondly, another closet containing a wash-hand basin, jug, towels, and other articles of toilet. The bureau and second closet are made to open at the end of the frame, the front surface of that part of the latter being formed with false drawers to correspond in appearance with the doors of the closet on the other side of the space ... Another part of the invention consists in constructing a music stool which is so arranged that in addition it contains a work-box, a looking-glass, a writing desk or table, and a small set of drawers.

The sheer cosiness of the idea might almost have been conceived as an antidote to one of the most popular and time-hardened branches of the domestic keyboard repertoire. Ever since Tudor times, composers had occasionally amused themselves and their patrons by depicting celebrated battles. By the end of the eighteenth century and the beginning of the next, however, the pastime had become a craze. Parlours on both sides of the Atlantic resounded to the thrill and thunder of literally hundreds of battlescapes, yet despite their proliferation these sonorous dramas showed an extraordinary similarity. Indeed pieces purporting to depict quite different engagements were often identical, the reasons being eminently logical.

Since battles, by their very nature, arouse and appeal to patriotic feelings, it stood to reason that the same piece of music couldn't be marketed with equal profit on both sides of the fence under the same title. One side's victory, after all, was another's defeat. Consequently, the titles were carefully contrived to arouse only pride in the player. What eighteenth-century Austrian, for instance, could be expected to resist a title so laden with historical significance as this?

THE BATTLE OF WÜRZBURG
on the Third of September, 1796,
between the royal Imperial Army under the command
of His Royal Highness the Archduke of Austria,
Imperial Field Marshal, and the *Enemy* French troops
under the command of General Jourdain.
A MILITARY AND HEROIC PIECE OF MUSIC

for
Clavier or Pianoforte
reverently dedicated to
KARL OF AUSTRIA
IMPERIAL FIELD MARSHAL
on the occasion of his glorious birthday
by the undersigned firm, and composed according to
the official Vienna communiqué of 8th September 1796
by
MR JOHANN WANHAL

If Herr Wanhal really did compose his piece according to the official Vienna communiqué, he was a more responsible historian than a certain Bohemian who marketed exactly the same piece, with great success, as *The Naval Battle and Total Destruction of the Dutch Fleet by Admiral Duncan, October 11, 1797, The Battle of Austerlitz* and more simply, *Le Combat Naval, or 'Battle at Sea'* (clearly aimed at neutral countries with a yen for vicarious excitement). In fact the selfsame piece surfaced again a few years later, this time commemorating *The Battle of Copenhagen.* But who was to know, much less care? Like the bullets they set out to emulate, these pieces went in one ear and out the other. But my, what a din they made in between. The composer often rallied his troops with specific instructions as to the handling of the artillery. Even as early as 1724, François Dandrieu, a church organist no less, issued the following command:

> In that section of the *Caractères de la Guerre* which I call 'The Charge', there are several places named 'cannon shots' that are indicated only by four notes forming a complete chord. But in order better to express the noise of the cannon, the player should, each time, in place of the four notes, strike the lowest notes of the keyboard with the entire length of the flat of the hand.

Almost a century later, a German composer, too, left no doubt that his intentions transcended the limits of mere notation:

The cannon shots are to be expressed by the flat of the left hand upon the lowest portion of the bass, all at once, and *loud*; all the notes are to be struck without distinction – and to be held until the final dying of the sound.

Not to be outdone by these lily-livered one-handers, a Frenchman by the name of Bernard Viguerie conscripted both hands at once in his deafening *Battle of Maringo*, in which they are brutally ordered to flatten the entire lower third of the keyboard.

The most famous and durable of these battlescapes by far was *The Battle of Prague*, composed in 1790 by an otherwise obscure Bohemian, František Kotzwara, who hanged himself in a London brothel with no inkling of the posthumous fame that awaited him. Indeed in the United States and throughout the British Empire this noisy but undistinguished warhorse was to become, for more than half a century, the best known and most frequently played of all extended piano works, blasting its way even into Windsor Castle, where it was applauded (and perhaps secretly played?) by Queen Victoria herself.

Generally speaking, however, these battle pieces were the equivalent of pulp fiction, of the kind that used to be described as 'penny dreadfuls', and they were frankly aimed at the parlour rather than the salon. But the fad for militaristic music, which rumbled on from roughly the middle of the eighteenth century to the middle of the nineteenth, was not without its compensations. To it we owe the well-known *Rondo alla turca* in Mozart's A major Sonata, K331, and the three delightful *Marches militaires* composed by Schubert for piano duet [CD 2]. Here we have the face of domestic music making at its most cosy and convivial. It was Mozart who raised the piano duet to the status of a high art form (his last two duet sonatas being comparable in quality with his great symphonies), but in this territory it was Schubert who really cornered the market. His many piano duets range from the briefest and most unassuming country dances (particularly the Ländler and waltzes, but also many delightful Écossaises) to the great F minor Fantasy which marks the summit of the medium.

The waltz in particular was just entering its heyday in Schubert's time and was still emphatically a dance to be danced to (the notion of the idealized 'concert' waltz then being in its infancy). How different from the great waltzes of Chopin, which followed on only a few years after Schubert's death in 1828. With very few exceptions, the waltzes of Chopin's French years are sparklingly extroverted affairs, shamelessly ingratiating (seldom has music been more evidently written to please), pianistically elegant and emotionally refined. Shrewdly designed for the ears of Parisian salonistes and the fingers of the more advanced dilettantes, they assured Chopin's success both socially and commercially, and more perhaps than any of his other works have enjoyed an unflagging popularity from his day to our own. That they have survived the surfeit of dross which once threatened to submerge the bourgeoisie of five continents is due entirely to the art which lies behind them, and to their Mozartian reflection of hidden depths beneath the surface. That the A minor, Chopin's own favourite [CD2], should ever have been published as a 'Grande valse brillante' is a perfect example of nineteenth-century commercialism at its crassest, the only accurate term in the title being 'valse'. Grand it emphatically isn't, and its 'brilliance' lies wholly in the genius which contains tragedy within the bounds of fashion. In spirit and technique, it lies closer to Mozart's equally subtle Rondo in the same key, and like that work requires restraint, variety and technical control in equal measure if it isn't to sound merely coy.

'Piano lessons': Victorian image of two girls at the piano (photograph c. 1857).

If the A minor is unique in character among Chopin's waltzes, it is wholly characteristic in its refinement. With a handful of un-important exceptions, Chopin made no qual-itative distinction between 'light' music and any other. He lavished almost as much care on outwardly frivolous pieces as on his most cherished and hard-wrung works. He also had the happy knack, when writing for the amateur market, of composing quite undemanding music, pianistically speaking, which nevertheless gave the impression of difficulty, even of virtuosity. The first two waltzes of Op. 64 offer excellent examples of this. The first, in D flat (misleadingly nicknamed the 'Minute' Waltz) owes much of its great popularity to this very fact. The almost equally popular C sharp minor is both fashionably wistful and genuinely profound,

A 1908 song-card for Arthur Sullivan's 'The Lost Chord'.

and though it may sound less brilliant is actually the more difficult of the two to play [CD 2].

Far removed from the strains of the aristocratic Parisian salon, with its galaxy of intelligentsia, was a form of music which flourished for some decades in Anglo-Saxon climes. In Victorian England, as in her former colony across the water, the most popular agent of domestic crowd control was the after-dinner ballad. The participants in these affairs were not, on the whole, professional musicians brought in from outside but enthusiastic if not particularly accomplished amateurs, drawn from the assembled company or the hosts' family. The songs themselves were generally sentimental numbers of polite character but little substance, far removed from the world of the true art song (further removed, indeed, than their most socially ambitious exponents liked to imagine). The piano accompaniments, on the whole, were such that any moderately accomplished daughter could play them without too much difficulty. Interestingly, their composers, like the bulk of their *ad hoc* accompanists, were often women, but their singers were predominantly male. Perhaps the most famous of these drawing-room ballads was *The Lost Chord* by Sir Arthur Sullivan, which sold some 500,000 copies in England alone.

Singing, of course, however engrossing the ballad, can be an awful trial if not done well. In some homes it was decided, therefore, to employ the services of a professional reciter who would simply declaim the ballad, leaving the musical side of the drama to the household pianist. The standard was sometimes quite high, as witness Schumann's *Ballads for Declama'ion* and Richard Strauss's splendid, over-the-top setting of Tennyson's *Enoch Arden*, memorably recorded in 1961 by Glenn Gould and Claude Rains. The latter, however, belongs more properly to the realm of *melodrama* as initiated by Jean-Jacques Rousseau in his *Pygmalion* of 1762, and is exemplified at its most effective by Beethoven in the dungeon scene of *Fidelio* and Weber in the Wolf's Glen scene in *Der Freischütz*. Early in the twentieth century a wide range of such melodramas for speaker and piano was readily available for domestic use on both sides of the Atlantic.

It is important to remember that before the advent of radio, television and video-recorders, it was music more than anything else that kept us entertained in company. Nor are the reasons hard to find. Quite apart from its highest attributes, it helped to pass the time. So did reading books or doing needlework or playing word-games, of course, but these were generally solitary pursuits. There were other, theoretically more companionable activities – card playing, charades and other parlour games – but these were laden with dangers. Games, being essentially competitive, too often bring out the worst in us. And ever conversation had its attendant risks. If it was to be general, and involve the whole company, it demanded a measure of attention, a modicum of thought, and sometimes more than a little self-control. It had as well, as it still has, an unnerving way of drying up, suddenly, leaving the company staring ruminatively into their wine glasses or leading to potentially embarrassing indiscretions. Music, then, among its other charms, was a handy antidote to conversation. Those who made it were kept occupied; those who listened were at least preoccupied. Of all known forms of domestic distraction, music was the safest;

and by the time the eighteenth century drew to a close, the piano, on both sides of the Atlantic, was rapidly becoming its most popular agent. By the onset of the twentieth its dominance was complete. The American writer Ambrose Bierce spoke for many when defining it in his *Devil's Dictionary* of 1906:

> PIANO, (noun). A parlor utensil for subduing the impenitent visitor. It is operated by depressing the keys of the instrument and the spirits of the audience.

Spirits were apt to sink still further with the inevitable after-dinner ballad. A frequent victim was Samuel Taylor Coleridge, who reflected ruefully,

> Swans sing before they die; 'twere no bad thing
> Should certain persons die before they sing.

It would be nice, but mistaken, to believe that Coleridge was speaking up, where home-made music was concerned, for the silent majority. The truth is, however, that the majority of drawing-room auditors were seldom silent. For those who wore their culture like a tiara, music was employed not so much as an antidote as an accompaniment to conversation, a fact readily acknowledged by an anonymous 'member of the aristocracy' in a Victorian book of etiquette: 'When music is given at afternoon "at homes", it is usual to listen to the performance – or at least to appear to do so; when conversation is carried on, it should be done in a low tone so as not unduly to disturb or annoy the performers.'

Nor was this merely an Anglo-American aberration. In eighteenth-century Austria, Germany and France, no less a figure than Mozart was frequently obliged to endure the same consideration on the part of continental aristocrats. So were such parlour piano favourites as Mendelssohn and Grieg, both excellent performers, much of whose music was tailor-made for genteel domestic consumption. Indeed the runaway success of Mendelssohn's *Songs without Words* largely eclipsed his most interesting and important piano works for the best part of a

Carl Czerny (1791–1857), from an engraving by Carl Mayer.

century: the *Variations sérieuses* for instance, a work in which he seems deliberately to distance himself from the froth and frivolity of the money-spinning variation merchants centred in Paris (hence the French title). Other substantial and unjustly neglected works are the Fantasia in F sharp minor, with its brilliant and exciting finale, the *Scherzo a capriccio* in the same key, and the captivating early Piano Sonata in E. The only substantial Mendelssohn piano work never to have suffered a moment's neglect is the *Andante and Rondo Capriccioso*, Op. 14. Combining his own very special brand of lyricism with his equally characteristic virtuoso style, it was composed when he was all of 15.

* * *

With the rapid proliferation of eager, would-be pianists came a commensurate proliferation of teachers ready to oblige them with instruction – whose number swelled progressively as their erstwhile pupils became teachers themselves. In 1800, Vienna alone, not one of the larger cities, harboured several hundred piano teachers. Most have long since receded into the mists of time but some left a posthumous influence which can still be felt today – none more so than the traditional bugbear of piano pupils everywhere, Carl Czerny (1791–1857).

A pupil of Hummel, Clementi and Beethoven, Czerny was one of the most industrious musicians who ever lived. Despite a busy teaching schedule (his pupils, incidentally, included both Thalberg and Liszt), he composed a fantastic amount of music, most of which has fallen into oblivion – not all of it deservedly. In addition to his string quartets, concertos, masses and many other works, he published 861 opus numbers of music for piano alone, each of which contained many individual pieces. He was also a busy arranger with a taste for extravagance which was nowhere evident in his lifestyle. His arrangement of Rossini's *William Tell* Overture calls for 16 pianists playing four-hands on eight pianos, and for that deprived multitude who boasted but one piano per household, Czerny could provide alternative arrangements for only three pianists playing six-hands on a single keyboard. As befitted a man of such prodigious output, he had several writing desks in his study, each supporting a different work in progress. While the ink dried on one, he would move on to the next desk, thus becoming music's first one-man assembly line.

Given this fact, and his evident partiality to the multi-piano jamboree, it comes as something of a surprise that it was not Czerny but another man who first applied similar industrial principles to the teaching of music. It was in 1814 that Johann Bernhard Logier, a German-born pianist, composer and bandmaster of whom we shall hear more, became the world's first assembly-line piano teacher, having devised an ingeniously lucrative system for instructing whole roomfuls of aspiring virtuosos simultaneously, knocking off as many as 20 in one go. Although his methods provoked heated controversy, they enjoyed a considerable vogue in England, Germany, France and the United States well into the nineteenth century.

Such was the popularity, even veneration, of the piano and its associated glories that no opprobrium attached to the profession of teacher. On the contrary: every musical person in the Paris of the 1830s knew that Chopin, like many of his most celebrated colleagues, was engaged as a teacher from morning to early evening. George Bernard Shaw's wicked contention that 'Those who can do; those who can't, teach', whatever its validity elsewhere, simply didn't apply. The popular Henri Herz, for instance, already wealthy from his conspicuous and sustained successes as both performer and composer, was altogether indefatigable as a teacher, pupils sometimes having to be slotted into his busy schedule at five o'clock in the morning.

The three greatest teachers of the nineteenth century, Franz Liszt,

An advertisement for piano lessons.

Theodor Leschetizky and Clara Schumann, confined themselves with few exceptions to professional pianists and thus had relatively little impact on the life of the piano in the home.

An interesting latterday complement to Logier's teaching factories was an experiment carried out in the 1920s by the Baldwin Piano and Organ Company in America. At their 'Electropiano Laboratories' up to two dozen pupils could play and practise simultaneously, their efforts heard only through individual sets of headphones and monitored by a solitary teacher positioned in the 'Control Center', where he could home in on any student, or all of them, as the circumstances warranted. But by then the role of the domestic piano was in sharp decline, and the experiment died from malnutrition.

CHAPTER 5

Lions and Lionizers

The piano, like the Romantic movement which it came in many ways to represent, was a child of revolution. Its rapid ascendancy, half a century after its birth, coincided with the American War of Independence and the earliest rumblings of the French Revolution. It scored its final triumph over the harpsichord during the period of the Napoleonic Wars, and came of age in the wake of the pan-European revolutions of 1848. Its centrality to the Romantic movement, however, had more to do with the Industrial Revolution than with any political upheavals. The harnessing of steam power in England in the last quarter of the eighteenth century and the consequent mechanization of the cotton and woollen industries led to mass markets for manufactured goods, a dramatic increase in economic opportunities and a concomitant increase in urban populations – a pattern soon to be repeated on the continent. The nineteenth century brought exciting discoveries in the study of electricity, and the progressive mechanization of heavy industry, with iron and steel works the major beneficiaries, transformed the face of international trade (let alone the manufacturing of pianos).

By the 1830s there was hardly a country in Europe that hadn't in some measure felt the breath of change. With the kings of the earth being toppled or dispossessed and humanity increasingly triumphant over nature, the very King of Heaven himself was called into question as never before – and well before Darwin. In certain respects the high tide of Romanticism marked the apex of man's love affair with himself (women can be absolved of this particular manifestation of vanity). It was a time for heroes, and of hero worship, Byronic and otherwise. Nor is it any accident that the musicians most lionized in this period were pianists. The piano itself, increasingly a product of the factory rather than the skilled craftsman, was a potent symbol of the machine age, a triumph of technology whose elaborate complexity and

SIG.ᴿ PAGANINI.

During one of his Performances at the King's Theatre.
June 1831.

London, Published July 12.ᵗʰ 1831 by W.ᵐ Spooner 259 Regent Street Oxford St.

The virtuoso violinist Niccolò Paganini pictured during a performance at the King's Theatre, June 1831 (lithograph). Paganini (1782–1840) exerted a huge influence on piano technique, both by example and by transcriptions of his works.

commercial success had themselves become objects of worship. Small wonder, then, that this particular conjunction of man and machine so fired the Romantic imagination. Still smaller wonder that the greatest hero figure to arise from it was an Adonis of incandescent virility and power – a superman of the keyboard whose feats had no precedent. Or to be more precise, no precedent but one.

Strange to say, the man who exerted the most formative influence on the piano music of the mid-nineteenth century was not himself a pianist, but a violinist. Indeed if Schubert, Liszt, Chopin, Schumann, Rossini and Berlioz are to be believed, he was very probably the greatest violinist who ever lived. So prodigious were his accomplishments that he was widely believed to have made a pact with the devil (some averred with unruffled credulity that he was the devil himself). On two composers in particular, the influence of Niccolò Paganini was decisive, and neither played the violin at all. On hearing the Demon Fiddler, both men resolved, quite independently, that they would do for the piano what Paganini had done for the violin: to reveal its very soul, discovering in it hitherto untapped resources and achieving heights of virtuosity never previously imagined. One was Chopin, the other was Liszt, and neither had yet achieved the age of 20.

Both were already among the greatest pianists in the world, and their immediate reactions to the Italian wizard could hardly have been more different. Chopin, who seems never to have experienced the slightest technical difficulty at the keyboard, responded almost entirely as a composer. Interestingly, too, his only piece formally commemorating Paganini is a sweet, innocuous little meditation on *The Carnival of Venice* – a valuable reminder that Paganini's lyrical playing was as remarkable as his virtuosity. (Schubert had likewise been impressed by this.) Liszt, on the other hand, went straight to the keyboard and scarcely left it. Already a virtuoso of unsurpassed achievements, he now settled down to a daily regimen of 14 hours, up to five of these being devoted entirely to exercises (thirds, sixths, octaves, tremolos, repeated notes, cadenzas and so on). As with Paganini, however, Liszt's fantastic power as a performer was only partly the result of his unprecedented technique. His purely musical genius was plainly overwhelming. Add to this his extravagant good looks and a charisma unique in musical history and you have a man who, even on the basis of hearsay, can be safely described as the greatest pianist who ever lived.

Liszt's public appearances were never forgotten by those who heard him, nor their aftermath by the man himself. Only slightly atypical was the response to his first concert in Budapest after an absence of many years. When Liszt left the hall to return to his hotel he was confronted by a spectacle that gave a whole new meaning to the word ovation.

> There was an immense crowd filling the square, and 200 young people, with lighted torches and a military band at their head, shouting 'Éljen! Éljen!' – the Hungarian for 'Vivat!'. Even at 11 o'clock in the evening, all the streets were full, and the shouts went on unceasingly. It is impossible to convey the enthusiasm, the respect and the love of this population!

It was Liszt more than anyone else who established the model on which the life of the concert pianist is based to this day. It was he who pioneered the solo recital (as he also invented its curious name). He was the first to play whole programmes from memory, the first to embrace the entire keyboard literature, as then known, the first consistently to place the piano at right angles to the platform, so that its opened lid projected the sound outwards towards the audience, and the first to play for gatherings of 3,000 and more.*

---

*The solo recital as we know it today was a late arrival on the scene, not establishing itself firmly until the middle of the nineteenth century. Concerts prior to that time were high-class variety acts in which it was not unusual for a symphony to be dismembered and delivered piecemeal, interspersed with songs, instrumental solos, vocal quartets, operatic arias and so on. The violinist Franz Clement has gone down in history not primarily because he gave the first performance of the Beethoven Violin Concerto but because in the process he entertained the audience by such edifying feats as playing on one string with the fiddle turned upside down.

Franz Liszt (1811–86) learnt from the virtuoso technique and flamboyant performing manner of Paganini. Painting by C. E. R. H. Lehmann, 1839.

Liszt's power to affect people – as a performer, as a musician, as a man – was phenomenal almost beyond belief. His recitals in Berlin in the early 1840s are a case in point, quite apart from the fact that they entailed 21 concerts and 80 works in the space of ten weeks. When he left the city, it was, in the words of the critic Ludwig Rellstab, 'not *like* a king, but *as* a king'.

> A carriage drawn by six white horses waited for him at his hotel. Amid much shouting and cheering, Liszt was practically carried down the steps and into the carriage, where he took his place next to the elders of the University. Thirty carriages-and-four, packed with students, followed his, escorted by 51 horsemen in academic gala array, and scores of private coaches joined the cavalcade, while thousands swarmed around the scene on foot. Even the court had ridden into town to witness this celebration of joy, and all the windows along the way were filled with cheering spectators.

Such reactions, however, were not confined to women, youths and sycophants. The eminent Russian critic Stasov – no pushover at the best of times – counted himself amongst the greatest sceptics prior to Liszt's debut in Russia. Afterwards, he succumbed entirely.

> We had never in our lives heard anything like this; we had never been in the presence of such brilliant, passionate, demonic temperament, at one moment rushing like a whirlwind, at another pouring forth cascades of the tenderest beauty and grace. Liszt's playing was absolutely over-whelming. After the concert, Serov and I were like two madmen. We exchanged only a few words and then rushed home to write down as quickly as possible our impressions, our dreams, our ecstasies. Then and there we took a vow that thenceforth and forever, that day, 8 April 1842, would be sacred to us, and we would never forget a single second of it till our dying day.

It should not be thought, however, that Liszt as a pianist was without his detractors. Unlike most virtuosos of his time, he publicly championed the works of other composers, but he often showed scant regard for the printed text, sometimes virtually recomposing the music on the spot, embroidering it with all manner of embellishments, pedal

Liszt performing for Emperor Franz Joseph in Budapest, 1872. Oil painting by Schams and Lafitte, 1872.

effects, contrapuntal variations and so on. 'Liszt can't keep his hands off anything,' said Clara Schumann, who abhorred him. And later: 'Before Liszt, people used to play. After Liszt they pounded or whispered. He has the decline of piano-playing on his conscience.'

Liszt gave his last concert in September 1847, and then astonished the musical world by announcing his retirement from the concert platform. He was 35 years old and at the very peak of his powers. From that time until his death just under 40 years later, he devoted himself to composing, conducting and teaching. He did, in fact, play in public again, but never for money – nor did he ever accept a penny from his many pupils, who included several of the greatest pianists of the century, among them Hans von Bülow, Feruccio Busoni, Eugen d'Albert, Moritz Rosenthal, Isaac Albeniz, Emil von Sauer and Karl Tausig.

In view of the reactions detailed above, it might seem inconceivable that Liszt as a pianist had any rivals, but he did. Chopin was in almost

every way too different to be called a rival, and in any case he fought
shy of public concerts. In the public sphere, there was only one man
who challenged Liszt's supremacy, and unlike Chopin he was prepared
to meet Liszt on his own terms. The lady who engineered this eagerly
awaited showdown (a direct descendant of the Mozart–Clementi battle
half a century earlier and a musical forerunner of the gunfight at the
O. K. Corral) was among the more colourful denizens of Parisian
high society.

Princess Cristina Belgiojoso was an Italian aristocrat of pronounced
republican sympathies. From her beautiful residence in the Faubourg
St Honoré she financed political insurgency in her native land and lent
lavish support to a number of musicians and writers. An accomplished
amateur pianist, she enshrouded herself in a mist of excessive sensibility, proceeding from rooms decorated with black velvet and studded
with silver stars to the Opéra, where, dressed in the habit of a nun,
but with lilies in her hair, she would allow herself to succumb so
intensely to the powers of music that she had frequently to be carried,
with insouciant conspicuousness, from her box to an awaiting carriage.
She was widely known, and not flatteringly, as the Romantic Muse. It
was for the benefit of her beloved Italian refugees that she persuaded
both Liszt and Sigismond von Thalberg to appear in competition at
her salon on 31 March 1837, thus scoring one of the greatest social
coups in history.

Despite a lifelong pretence of noble illegitimacy (he claimed to be
the illicit offspring of Count Moritz von Dietrichstein and the Baroness
von Wetzlar), Thalberg's birth certificate establishes him as the son of
Joseph Thalberg and Fortunée Stein of Frankfurt. Although lionized
in his day as one of the greatest virtuosos of all time, he is remembered
by posterity almost exclusively for his rivalry with Liszt. And apart
from their virtuosity and cult status (especially among women), the
two could hardly have been less alike. Where Liszt was flamboyant
and extravagantly gymnastic at the keyboard, Thalberg was the very
picture of dignified restraint, the ultimate gentleman, courteous but
detached, charming but not ingratiating, confident but serene, and

like Chopin, always immaculately groomed and elegantly dressed.*

Unlike Liszt or Chopin, Thalberg had a trademark: a technique of dividing a melody between the two hands (mainly the two thumbs), and surrounding it with sweeping arpeggios, giving the impression of three independent hands. It was an idea briefly adopted by Mendelssohn and Schumann and seems to have been modelled originally on the playing of the harpist Parish Alvars. The illusion was reinforced by the publication of Thalberg's music on three staves. Like Mendelssohn, Thalberg, for all his bravura, was essentially a classicist, renowned for his impeccable clarity of tex-

Sigismond Thalberg (1812–71), Liszt's greatest rival at the piano.

ture (illumined by an exquisite harmonic wash entrusted mainly to the pedals, of which he was a consummate master). Like most pianists of the day he seldom played anything but his own music. On the few occasions when he did, he showed an almost twentieth-century respect for the composer's text, far removed from Liszt's creative abandon as an interpreter.

Among Thalberg's greatest accomplishments as a pianist was a suppleness of line which wholly belied the essentially percussive nature of the piano. His particular manner of unfurling long, sumptuous melodies was something never heard before, and drew praise even

---

*He told Ignaz Moscheles 'that he had acquired his posture and self-control by smoking a Turkish pipe while practising his exercises; the length of the tube being so calculated as to keep him erect and motionless'.

from his adversary Liszt: 'Thalberg,' he wrote, 'is the only man who can play the violin on the piano.' Unsurprisingly, when Thalberg came to write his own *méthode*, as was the custom of the time, he entitled it *The Art of Singing Applied to the Piano*. With such witnesses as Mendelssohn, Berlioz, Robert and Clara Schumann, and the formidable scholar–critic Fétis, it seems fair to say that he was widely regarded, at the very highest level, as Liszt's equal. Small wonder, then, that he was the most expensive soloist of his day. He was also one of the most indefatigable. In the season following his New York debut in 1856, he played 56 concerts in New York alone, often squeezing three appearances into a single day. Wherever he played, he was extravagantly received – never more so than in Boston, Massachusetts, where the critic of *The Boston Post* succumbed to a perfect paroxysm of purple prose:

> Rarely has the omni-ambient aether pervading the purlieus of the palatial metropolis vibrated resonant to more majestic music, to more soothing strains, than sought the cerulean empyrean vault, 'as the bee flieth,' on Saturday morn from the digitals of the gifted Sigismond.

Thalberg retired, a rich man, in 1863, thereafter pursuing the life of a leisured Italian wine-grower. So entirely did he turn his back on music that he didn't even have a piano in the house. If he survives in history as little more than a footnote, it must be put down to the relative poverty of his music, although even here he attracted some very distinguished admirers, improbably including Schumann who was in general implacably opposed to everything Thalberg stood for. The few efforts made in the twentieth century to revive interest in Thalberg's music have failed, and his complete abandonment of music in retirement suggests that he knew his time was over.

In this, as in most other respects, he could hardly have been more different from Chopin, who both as a composer and a pianist was a law unto himself. When Liszt the composer remarked, in his later years, that it was his intention 'to hurl a lance into the indefinite reaches of the future' he must have known, though he failed to say so, that Chopin's lance had got there first. In the entire history of music there is perhaps no instance of a composer, or pianist, more prophetic of things to come.

To describe Chopin as a lion of the keyboard would be misleading on two counts, first because he abhorred public concerts and seldom played loudly enough to reach the back gallery of a large hall, and secondly because his style of playing, while undoubtedly feline in character, was never kingly, never cast in the heroic mould. Grandeur, strength and tonal splendour, let alone gladiatorial confrontation, were never among his chief attributes as a performer. Grace, speed and suppleness of rhythm, on the other hand, were. If he was a cat, it was a cheetah, a panther or a leopard, not a lion. As a composer, he was largely dependent on the piano for his ideas. To an exceptional degree, he was a musician who thought with his fingers. In no composer's work are sound and gesture more inextricably combined. The tactile element in Chopin's music is paramount, yet while he was undoubtedly a sensualist he was never a voluptuary. As a poet he stood closer to Keats than to Byron. He was an aesthete but never a poseur.

Frédéric Chopin (1810–49). Oil painting after the portrait by Ary Scheffer.

Unlike Liszt, his almost exact contemporary and sometime friend, Chopin as a pianist – indeed Chopin as a composer – was in most respects fully formed by the time he reached official manhood. When at the age of 21 he arrived in Paris from his native Poland, he was already one of the two or three greatest pianists of his time. Many if not indeed most of his epoch-making Études were already composed. As a pianistic painter he had no rivals. His command of tone colour was of a subtlety and resourcefulness hitherto undreamt of, and probably unequalled until the emergence of Debussy at the latter end of the century. His rhythm, too, combined unprecedented sophistication with the primitive complexity of Polish folk music. The subtlety and variety of his *rubato* (the expressive displacement of rhythm from its unwavering metrical path), left his listeners speechless with wonder. He took unprecedented liberties with

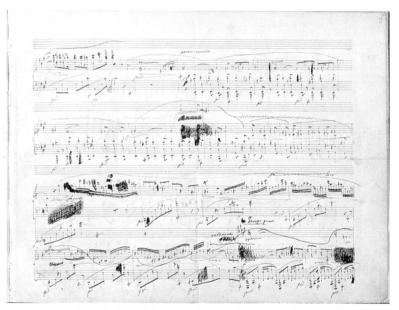

A section from the MS of Chopin's Barcarolle in F sharp major, Op. 60 (1845–6).

his inflection of melody yet never deviated from the strictest observance of the underlying metrical pulse. In this, as in many other respects, he was remarkably close to the expressed 'Classical' ideal of his revered Mozart, though Chopin cannot possibly have known the now famous letter in which Mozart spells it out.

As in his composition, so in his playing, Chopin was one of music's greatest originals. No one previously had written for the piano as

Chopin Elisa Radziwill Prinzessin Luise
Fürst Anton Radziwill Wanda Radziwill A. von Humboldt

Friedrich Chopin im Salon des Fürsten Anton Radziwill (1829).
Ölgemälde von H. Siemiradzki.

Concert given by Chopin in the Salon of Prince Anton Radziwill, 1829, after a painting by Hendrik Siemiradzki.

Chopin did, nor had they played it as he did. The flexibility of his hands, the looseness of his wrists, the balletic grace and suppleness of his arms, all these introduced something quite new to the concept of piano technique.* Despite his fabled (and much exaggerated) physical weakness he could play for hours on end without showing the slightest fatigue. Stiffness and muscular tension were unknown to him. '*Souplesse!*' he would say to his students, '*souplesse avant tout!*' (Suppleness! Suppleness before everything!). And though he wrote some of the most hair-raisingly difficult music ever composed, the most frequent adverb

---

*Stephen Heller recalled how Chopin's hands would 'suddenly expand and cover a third of the keyboard, like the opening of the mouth of a serpent about to swallow a rabbit whole'.

in his teaching vocabulary was '*facilement*' (easily). In whatever Chopin played there was an uncanny sense of immediacy, of freshness, of music being conjured out of the air. No man ever more magically transcended the mechanical nature of the piano than Chopin. His beautiful, arching, continuous unfurling of melody was comparable with the greatest opera singers, who influenced him far more than any pianist ever did. More particularly, he animated to a unique degree and in an entirely inimitable fashion the phenomenon of melody as the surface of harmony. His melodies floated not like objects in the sea but like sunlight on the ever-shifting contour of the waves. And so they continue to do in his music – witness, among many other things, the so-called 'Aeolian Harp' Étude which opens his second great set, Op. 25. Here we find melody, undoubtedly, but strip away the harmony and you have scarcely any tune.

The same could hardly be said of his perennially popular Nocturnes, whose melodies in their extraordinary flexibility seem to defy the very nature of the piano. Ironically, his greatest nocturne, by common consent, goes by another name, and it brings us as close to programme music as Chopin ever allowed himself to get. His unique *Barcarolle*, Op. 60 (unforgettably played by Artur Rubinstein on CD 2), is the greatest of all Venetian boat songs, from the very first bar, in which the gondolier may be imagined pushing his craft out into the water. Nowhere does the fastidious Chopin come closer to the intense sensuality that Wagner was later to achieve in his *Tristan und Isolde*, where the act of love is unmistakably played out in sound. Although he wrote almost exclusively for solo piano, Chopin's range as a composer was fantastic. His many mazurkas retain their captivating strangeness and downright modernity even today, his waltzes are at the very least the apotheosis of musical confectionery, his ballades and scherzos are musical dramas of extraordinary power and originality, and his two great sonatas (discounting an early, prentice work) traverse a dramatic terrain almost symphonic in scope.

Whenever and wherever he performed in public, there was one persistent criticism made of Chopin's playing and that was that he didn't play loudly enough. For generations it has been put about that he didn't play louder because he couldn't play louder. True, he was slight (five foot two and roughly a hundred pounds at his healthiest), but the fact is that there are countless children smaller and lighter than that who can produce masses of volume on a modern concert grand, which is incomparably heavier to the touch than any instrument ever played by Chopin. The simple and illuminating truth is that Chopin didn't play louder because he didn't want to play louder. His ideal sound world, like Mozart's, was one in which stridency and steely-fingered power played no part, and on the pianos of his day these could only be avoided by dint of physical restraint. What mattered was the relative, not the absolute loudness of any given note. But Chopin's playing was hardly without drama. His uncanny control of the quietest regions of the piano enabled him to build the same pattern of contrasts and relationships, the same rhetorical and expressive use of accentuation as might be achieved by a more 'powerful' player. As a pianist Chopin was unique in his time, and those were luckiest who heard him in the relative intimacy of the aristocratic Parisian salons.

Chopin was only one of the many immigrants who contributed to the brilliance of Paris as the cultural capital of the world. Others drawn by its magnetic force included Heine, Liszt, Rossini, Bellini, Donizetti, Kalkbrenner, Cherubini, Hallé, Herz, Dreyschock – and a young arrival from the New World who was to leave a lasting imprint on the history of the piano and piano composition alike.

Refused an audition for the Paris Conservatoire in 1842 on the then fashionable grounds that he was an American, Louis Moreau Gottschalk survived the slight and three years later, now 16, is said to have been dubbed by Chopin the future 'king of pianists'. As a composer he made his mark before he was even 20 with such exotic reminiscences of his native New Orleans as *Bamboula*, *La Savane* and *La Bananier*, and came to be justifiably renowned as the first authentic musical spokesman of the New World. He became the musical idol of Spain, memorialized in such delightful and taxing numbers as *Souvenir*

A satire of Gottschalk's 'monster' concert: 56 pianists and 2 orchestras in the Teatro Lyrico Fluminense, Rio de Janeiro, October 1869.

d'Andalousie – the first piano piece ever to popularize the pungent styles of flamenco (discounting the sonatas of Scarlatti and the *Fandango* of Antonio Soler, which were written for the harpsichord).

He quickly became a favourite with the crowned heads of Europe, and his energies seem to have known no limit. In a single season (1850–51) he gave 75 concerts in Paris alone. Berlioz wrote of him:

> Gottschalk is one of the very small number who possess all the different elements of a consummate pianist, all the faculties which surround him with an irresistible prestige and give him sovereign power. There is an exquisite grace in his manner of phrasing sweet melodies and scattering the light passages from the top of the keyboard. The boldness, brilliancy and originality of his playing at once dazzle and astonish.

Gottschalk returned home in 1853 to a hero's welcome. In the New York *Tribune* of 12 February the critic William Henry Fry, who had spent some time in Europe and knew the musical scene well, proclaimed that Gottschalk combined 'the sublimity and grandeur of Thalberg with the beauty and finish of Liszt'. From a man who knew the playing of both, this was no idle praise.

After his father's death that year, Gottschalk became the breadwinner for his six younger brothers and sisters, touring extensively throughout the Americas and hitting the jackpot with a whole series of sentimental, semi-programmatic 'weepies', tailor-made for the genteel lachrymosity which was then the height of fashion. The most travelled pianist of his time, he covered hundreds of thousands of miles, giving thousands of recitals. He was the first of the piano's real matinée idols, and his love affairs and seductions became legendary. In 1865 he was forced to flee from his native land in the wake of a sexual scandal that titillated newspaper readers from coast to coast. With the vigilantes close on his heels, he set sail for South America, where after feverish activity (including the mounting of 'monster concerts' involving as many as 650 performers) he collapsed on stage while playing his own *Morte!!*, dying shortly thereafter, on 18 December 1869. Of his many compositions, *The Last Hope* and *The Dying Poet* scored the most sensational success,* but his importance lies in many far better pieces, such as the hugely enjoyable *Ojos Criollos* (Creole Eyes), which he once arranged for a record-breaking ensemble of 40 pianos, *Bamboula*, *Manchega*, *Le Mancenillier*, *La Gallina*, *Le Bananier* and a number of others, which anticipate many later features of American music with extraordinary prescience. Ragtime, jazz, the Latin Americana of Gershwin, Copland and Bernstein, the populist allusiveness of Ives and the American experimental tradition, all are prefigured in Gottschalk's piano music, and never more entertainingly than in *The Banjo*, a splendid, characterful showpiece, fully deserving of revival [CD 2].

---

* *The Last Hope* resonated tearfully in American parlours throughout the century, proving one of the all-time best-sellers in musical history, and *The Dying Poet* was still flourishing in the heyday of the silent cinema, where it proved a handy stand-by for all manner of films on both sides of the Atlantic.

With the outbreak of the American Civil War in 1861, Gottschalk took the side of the North. Although his father had been a slave owner, he himself was a passionate abolitionist. His diary, posthumously published as *Notes of a Pianist*, is a remarkable book from many points of view – an excellent read, full of fascinating observations, remarkably evocative scene paintings, extravagant adventures, and one of the most immediate accounts of the Civil War ever written.

Ultimately, Gottschalk can fairly be seen as a tragic figure who never fully rose to the challenge of his own gifts – a Peter Pan of the piano, trapped in a time warp from which he did nothing to escape. As one critic put it bluntly in 1862:

> Twenty-five years ago a concert player could amuse his audience for several years with six fantasias of his own make, and become famous on the strength of them. This has fortunately changed, although to judge from some features of the compositions of Mr Gottschalk, and the complacent consistency with which he adheres to them, we should think he is not aware of the change.

If he wasn't, then his head must have been buried very deeply in the sand. There had indeed been a sea-change in the pattern of concert life, on both sides of the Atlantic, and while generalizations are invariably simplistic, it can be attributed very largely to the influence of two men, one a German, the other a Russian.

Hans von Bülow was the first and for some considerable time the greatest of a new breed: the purely interpretative musician. As both pianist and conductor, he gave his life entirely to the music of others. No pianist of his time possessed a sharper intellect, a more formidable grasp of the keyboard and its possibilities – or a more abrasive personality. As a young man, he wrote to his mother, 'my unpopularity is unbounded – and I rejoice in it!' A rabid anti-Semite like his idol Wagner (who later stole his wife, Liszt's daughter Cosima), he believed utterly in the unassailable supremacy of German music and did more than any other musician to establish it as the very bedrock of the Western concert repertoire. Considering the cast, it can't have been all that difficult. What national tradition, after all, could match a line-up including Bach, Handel, Haydn, Mozart, Beethoven, Schubert, Weber, Schumann, Mendelssohn and Wagner; not to mention Liszt (Germanic in all but origin), Bruckner and Brahms?

A child prodigy, like most of the great pianists, he worked hard at the piano, but unlike most great pianists elected to go to university, where he studied law, wrote lengthy and scholarly political tracts, copious musical criticism of a largely polemical nature, and immersed himself in musical scores of every kind. He then became Liszt's pupil, whereupon he redoubled his pianistic endeavours with fanatical zeal. 'I devote the greater part of my time,'

Title page of Gottschalk's The Banjo.

he wrote, 'four or five hours daily, exclusively to the cultivation of technique. I make martyrs of the eventual founders of my material prosperity; I crucify, like a good Christ, the flesh of my fingers, in order to make them obedient, submissive machines to the mind, as a pianist must.'

With those martyred fingers he did indeed found his material prosperity, and a reputation which would long outlast him. In alliance with his penetrating intellect and a depth of musicianship rarely encountered, they saw him enthroned as one of the high priests of music. His authority was awe-inspiring. His repertoire encompassed almost everything but he became most famous as a Beethoven interpreter, and was known to play all of the last five sonatas (including the *Hammerklavier*, itself nearly an hour long) in a single programme. His performances were revelations, leaving his audiences thunderstruck. As one prominent critic put it, 'Those who wish to add

Hans von Bülow (1830–94),
married to Liszt's daughter
Cosima until she left him for
Wagner.

intellectual enjoyment to the pleasures of the imagination derive a happiness from Bülow's playing which no other pianist can give to the same degree.' Nor did any other pianist come onto the platform fully decked out with silk hat, cane and gloves, which he would ostentatiously remove before attending to the business of the evening. As he made his way to and from the piano at his historic recitals he regarded his spellbound audiences with undisguised contempt. Nor did he spare them his scorn during the performance. In the words of one observer, 'His expression is proud and supercilious to the last degree, and he looks all around at his audience when he is playing. His face seems to say "you are all cats and dogs and I don't care what you think of my playing"'.' He thought nothing of lecturing his audiences, or as the soloist in a concerto, of audibly disparaging conductor and orchestra alike. That his colleagues and admirers were prepared to put up with all this speaks volumes for his greatness as an interpreter. Indeed there was only one man who could challenge his supremacy across such a wide range of repertoire, and that man held the affection as well as the respect of his audiences.

Anton Rubinstein (not to be confused with his near-namesake Artur Rubinstein) is remembered today, if at all, as a legendary virtuoso, and by one or two piano pieces which crop up very occasionally in piano anthologies. There was a time, however, when his music was amongst the most popular ever written. Like his almost equally influential brother Nikolai (the first and most important director of the Moscow Conservatory), he was Russian-born but Western-trained, and much of what he brought to Russian music and musicians was imported from Europe – a fact which hardly endeared him to the increasingly powerful nationalist school, led by Balakirev and often referred to as 'The Mighty Handful' (its other members being Borodin, Mussorgsky, Rimsky-Korsakov and the now virtually forgotten César Cui). He was the first Russian to achieve equal status as pianist and composer, standing at the head of a tradition later upheld by such composer–pianists as Scriabin, Rachmaninov, Medtner and Prokofiev, and with his brother he did much to raise the standard of professionalism in Russian musical life, applying European methods of education and extolling the virtues of the great Germanic tradition. He was an especially renowned interpreter of Beethoven, of whom he was widely rumoured to be the illegitimate son (though this would have required of his mother a pregnancy of two and a half years) but was unusual for his time in detesting Wagner. Among his many compositions for

Silhouette (1886) of Anton Rubinstein at the piano.

POLICE PROTECTION FOR PIANISTS!!

MADE NECESSARY BY THE ANTICS OF THE PADDED-ROOMSKI DEVOTEES AT ST. JAMES'S HALL, WHO RUSH AT, TRY TO EMBRACE, AND DECK WITH ROSES, A CERTAIN MASTER WHENEVER HE APPEARS.

Cartoon of police protecting Paderewski – an early victim of musical groupies.

piano the most popular were the *Melody in F, Kammenoi-Ostrow* (The Rocky Island), the Piano Concerto No. 4 and the entrancingly exuberant *Valse-caprice.*

As a performer he was plainly phenomenal, and like Liszt, to whom many compared him, had charisma to burn, though he was by no means handsome. His technique was colossal – though accuracy often yielded to passion – his tonal palette was kaleidoscopic, his memory infallible up to his 50th year, and his stamina unique. Well before undertaking his legendary 'historical recitals' (a seven-concert cycle, given in many cities and covering the entire history of piano music), his programmes regularly ran to three hours and embraced as many as 20 works (not merely miniatures but a generous handful of major sonatas, such as Schumann's F sharp minor, Beethoven's 'Tempest' and A major Sonata, Op. 101). After each of these marathons, he would offer encores by the dozen, often including Chopin's B flat minor Sonata in its entirety. Regarded by many connoisseurs as the near-equal of Liszt, he attracted an almost fanatical following, not least in America, where in the 1872–3 season he gave 215 concerts in 239 days, sometimes giving as many as three in a single day, each one in a different city.

Although he was associated for some time with the Liszt circle in Weimar, Rubinstein was never, despite frequent claims to the contrary, one of the great man's pupils. But for all his imposing reputation and forbidding appearance, Rubinstein showed a Lisztian generosity to his colleagues and played a significant role in the early life of one who was to become the most lionized pianist after Liszt himself.

Ignace Jan Paderewski (1860–1941) had only two ambitions as a child. 'I want to be *somebody*,' he wrote, 'and I want to help Poland.' Both dreams were fulfilled beyond his highest hopes. But while he appears to have been born with a sense of destiny, he left nothing to chance. Encouraged early on as a composer, he had been actively warned off a career as a concert pianist. He simply hadn't the technique. There was, however, one dissenter from this view, and that was Rubinstein, who gave him every encouragement. A young man of destiny needed no more. At the late age of 24, he persuaded the renowned Theodor Leschetizky to accept him as a pupil. Beginning with simple finger exercises, he now worked at the piano with such obsessive tenacity that he would sometimes fall unconscious to the floor after practising for 11 or 12 hours at a stretch. In 1888 he made his debut in Paris. Thereafter, his career was meteoric. Within two years there was not a musical city in Europe where Paderewski wasn't a household name. By the time he made his American debut in 1891, his fabulous reputation had preceded him, prompting the quip by one critic present, 'He's good – but he's no Paderewski.'

There was far more to Paderewski's success, however, than music. His mere appearance on the platform was charisma incarnate, and his effect on women, in particular, was positively Lisztian. Wherever he went, he was besieged by groupies and pubescent autograph seekers, two of whom, armed with scissors, once pursued him through a San Francisco hotel hellbent on securing a lock of the great man's hair. Nor was his impact confined to the young. He remembered:

> One of the places where I had particular pleasure, and an especially unique experience in playing, was Bremen. I don't know why, but I hardly saw one young person there. They were all old people, and as

the concert went on they got so enthusiastic and excited that they began throwing hats and even umbrellas onto the platform as a mark of appreciation. They completely lost their heads. Anything they had, they threw on the platform, and it really became very dangerous. It was a veritable shower of missiles.

Paderewski was one of those rare figures who have only to enter a room in order for the atmosphere to change at once. His very presence had an inspiring effect on people, and his generosity was legendary. As the highest-paid performer in history,* it might cynically be said that he had plenty to be generous with, but wherever he went, it was his spirit not his cash that lingered in the memory. Well before his career as a statesman (he became the first Prime Minister of a newly independent Poland in 1919) he travelled with a kingly entourage, including his wife, his tuner, his manager, his valet, his doctor, and often his lawyer or some gilt-edged impresario. Nevertheless, the going could be rough. At the dawning of 1904, the Wright brothers' famous flight at Kitty Hawk was still hot news, and many countries had minimal railways, if railways at all. For Paderewski, who was touring New Zealand, one journey in particular was engraved on his memory.

> We travelled for hours and hours along an abyss. There were two rows of horses, and it was a rough, primitive road. On one side the mountains, on the other the abyss. There wasn't more than a foot between the carriage and a precipice some 2,000 feet deep. If one of those horses had slipped, we would have gone down – forever.

In the midst of this particularly gruelling tour, and as an antidote to the gloom which began to affect the entire party, Paderewski's agent presented him with a talking parrot – a generous act, but one which introduced a passing note of tension into the artist's marriage.

> It really was a rather unfortunate idea, for the bird made such an impression on my wife that she bought another 30 or 40, and we then travelled with a whole flock of birds of all kinds, ages, sizes and colours in a multitude of cages.

---

*In 1914 he netted the equivalent of £2,000,000 plus for a tour of 90 concerts.

Among this winged menagerie was one whose character and vocabulary set him apart from all others.

> Cocky Roberts talked almost without interruption and his vocabulary was extremely rich and very large. He regularly came to my room when I was practising. He would walk straight to the piano and perch there on my foot for hours. From time to time he would say in a very loving and scratchy voice, 'Lord, how beautiful! How beautiful!'

It was an opinion shared by many millions of music lovers all over the world.

By the time of his death in 1941 at the age of 80, Paderewski was a figure unique in the cultural, and indeed the political history of the West – a man whose generosity of spirit and firmness of purpose had made him a symbol of all that is best in a civilized world. A man, too, whose ennobling simplicity can still be heard through all the hiss and crackle of the records which he reluctantly made near the end of his long and unprecedented career.

Paderewski's repertoire was wide-ranging but his name will always be linked first and foremost with the music of his compatriot Chopin. The legacy of his recordings pre-

Unidentified caricature of Paderewski from an American newspaper, c. 1910.

sents a confusing picture ranging from the sublime to the mannered and mundane, even when allowances are made for the vast differences of style between his era and our own. It must be remembered when listening to these recordings, that the apparently stilted *rubato* and the intentional desynchronization of the hands were by no means peculiar to Paderewski but reflected the prevailing style of the time. Behind them, however, lie a deep-rooted artistry and an aristocratic poise seldom equalled before or since.

CHAPTER 6

Coming of Age

If Hummel and his teacher Clementi may be said to have represented the transition between the Classical and Romantic styles, their younger pupils and colleagues – Czerny, Kalkbrenner, Liszt, Thalberg, Herz – allied themselves firmly with the latter. They were by no means the first composer–pianists to write immensely difficult works for the piano, but in the emphasis they placed on bravura, on technical innovation and display for its own sake, they were very much the sons of their age.

For various reasons, among them the pervasive influence of Paganini and the growing interest in orchestral and operatic music, the piano music of this period is full of figures with repeated notes in imitation of the violin *tremolando*. And here pianists and composers were at least one step ahead of the manufacturers. In order to fulfil the requirements both of the new virtuoso style and the amateur craze for transcriptions and arrangements of operatic and orchestral works, an action was needed where the note could sound at two different levels of the key; that is to say where the key itself needn't rise to its full height in order to restrike. It was Sébastien Erard in Paris who achieved the breakthrough, in 1821, with an action combining a powerful stroke with a light flexible touch, giving the power to restrike any note with extreme rapidity. It was an epoch-making invention and forms the basis of virtually all 'double escapement' actions to this. day. More, it might be said to have provided the model on which the whole of modern piano technique was built. Its effect on the already booming market in piano arrangements was salutary to say the least. Throughout the nineteenth century, virtuosos from Liszt downwards disgorged hundreds of transcriptions, concert paraphrases, operatic fantasies and popular medleys. Nor had the fashion run its course by the onset of the twentieth century.

Of latterday practitioners, including such masters as Busoni, Reger, Debussy and Bartók, none exceeded the skill of Rachmaninov, whose dazzling arrangement of the Scherzo from Mendelssohn's *A Midsummer Night's Dream* got the performance of its life in 1939, recorded in one take by the great Benno Moiseiwitsch [CD 2].

By that time, the piano had long since attained its full maturity and it is doubtful whether even Erard with his revolutionary double escapement could have foreseen just how grand a grand piano could become. No one knew better than he that in the pianos of his own time there were more fundamental problems to be addressed than the rebounding of hammers, and they had been evident well before the turn of the century. Beginning with Beethoven and culminating in the 'heroic' style of Liszt in his best barnstorming vein, the eighteenth-century instrument so beloved of Mozart proved woefully inadequate to the demands being made of it.* But for many years, attempts to deal with the problem had only brought others in their wake. As pianos were fitted with more and heavier strings, keyboards of extended range, felt-covered hammers rather than the earlier leather-capped type, heavier actions and so on, the strain on the soundboard and the traditional wooden frame became intolerable.

Despite a widespread belief that the introduction of iron into the piano would impair the quality of tone, it was abundantly clear by the second decade of the nineteenth century that some form of metal frame was urgently needed to withstand the stress. Well before the complete iron frame became established, however, many manufacturers experimented with various sizes, shapes and constitutions of metallic braces, either solid bars or various lengths and diameters of tubing. Among the first pioneers of the fully integrated iron frame were Karl Röllig, who was experimenting with the idea as early as 1795, and Hawkins in Philadelphia who patented a metal frame in

*Liszt often had two pianos on the platform at once, so that one could be moved up whilst the damage inflicted on the first was being repaired by an attendant tuner.

Square piano by Jonas Chickering, 1850, showing its single continuous cast-iron frame.

1800. But it was Alpheus Babcock (1785–1842) who made history with his patenting in 1825 of the first full, single-cast metal frame, including the hitchpin plate or wrest plank. It was from this device that all subsequent developments of the cast-iron frame derived. In the story of its journey to perfection, a special place must be accorded to Jonas Chickering of Boston, whose single-cast grand piano frame of 1843 represents a significant landmark in the piano's evolution. One of the more interesting blind alleys in this sphere was Bachman's patent in 1850 for a piano with an iron soundboard.

Among the many works in which Liszt asked more of his pianos than it was theirs to give are the immense B minor Sonata (perhaps the greatest of all his works), the 'Dante' Sonata from his *Années de pèlerinage*, and a large percentage of his trailblazing Études. The most popular have always been the so-called *Hungarian Rhapsodies*, based not, as Liszt believed, on the indigenous folk tradition but on the heavily commercialized music of the Hungarian gypsies. Of these, No. 13 in A minor probably comes closest to its original model, with its slow, exotic, almost Middle Eastern opening section (the *Lassu* of the standard Hungarian *csárdás*) and its accelerating, unabashedly manipulative second part (the *Friss*). It would be hard to imagine a pianist better suited to its improvisatory abandon than Shura Cherkassky (1911–96), a former pupil of Josef Hofmann and one of the last links with the 'golden age' of pianism personified by Liszt himself [CD 2].

Liszt and Chopin, of course, were not the only pianist–composers to have been fundamentally affected by the playing of Paganini. Throughout Europe his influence inspired a generation of instrumentalists (more of them pianists than string players, interestingly) who became positively obsessed with technique. There was the young Alexander Dreyschock, who spent 16 hours a day practising the left hand alone, until he could play the whole of Chopin's so-called 'Revolutionary' Étude, up to speed, in octaves – a feat which beggars belief but is attested to by many witnesses. There was Adolf Henselt, who regularly practised 10 hours a day, largely concentrating on his extensions, which eventually encompassed C–E–G–C–F in the left hand and B–E–A–C–E in the right. Nor did he have large hands. Such was the strength of his fingers, however, that he could produce the most thunderous *fortissimos* using his fingers alone, with no movement of the hand, wrist or elbow. And there was Schumann, who crippled his right hand with a mechanical contrivance of his own devising, aimed at securing the independence of his fourth finger. But Schumann's recognition of Paganini took a more positive form in his musical composition

Robert Schumann (1810–56). Drawing by J. B. Laurens, 1853.

– works like the *Concert Studies on the Caprices of Paganini* or *Carnaval*, the best-known of his unique 'piano cycles'.* The fearsome Toccata in C, which he completed in 1833 (the same year as his Paganini studies), has proved a favourite with such sovereign virtuosos as Josef Lhévinne and Sviatoslav Richter, but its peculiarly obsessive, even diabolical qualities have never been more conspicuously revealed than in the recording made of it in 1934 by the twentieth century's most Paganinian pianist, Vladimir Horowitz [CD 2].

Although his career fell entirely within the twentieth century, Horowitz was in many ways a throwback to the heady days of the mid-nineteenth century, when pianists were often more lionized than the composers whose works they performed, or in some cases almost literally re-created. Save for his dates (1904–89), his natural place in the present volume would have been in Chapter 5. He was both lion and lionized to an extent unmatched by any of his close contemporaries, yet strange to say, it is just conceivable that if it hadn't been for the Russian Revolution we might never have heard him. Until the liquidation of his family's fortunes by the Bolsheviks in 1917, Horowitz had intended to devote his life to composition. According to his own testimony, it was financial pressure alone that drove him onto the concert platform. Seven years after the revolution, in the space of a single year, the 20-year-old Horowitz played no fewer than 25 separate recitals in Leningrad alone, without repeating a single work. In the following year, encouraged by Artur Schnabel, he left Russia for Germany, and it was there that the Horowitz legend was born. In only a little time, this slim, rather dandified youth was playing to sold-out houses of 3,000 and more, and in Paris he roused the audience to such a pitch of excitement that the police were called in to quell them. Almost from the beginning, his career and public persona were

---

* Other examples are the fantastical *Davidsbündlertänze* (Dances of the Band of David), *Kreisleriana* (based on a literary work by E. T. A. Hoffmann), *Papillons* (Butterflies), the *Humoreske* (not at all a humorous work) and the *Fantasiestücke*, Op. 12. He also wrote three very remarkable sonatas, but his greatest piano work, by general consent, is the three-movement Fantasia in C.

Top view of a Steinway grand piano with parallel stringing, 1857.

managed with all the calculating strategy of a military campaign. Increasingly, he pursued the lifestyle of a reclusive film star and nourished the image of himself as a magician whose secrets could never be unravelled. Nor did his marriage in 1933 to Toscanini's daughter do anything to diminish the glamour which surrounded him.

In one sense Horowitz was an old-fashioned Romantic, for whom the interpreter shared equal billing with the composer (he not only re-created but sometimes substantially rewrote certain works); in another sense he was (or tried to be) a simple, even humble servant of his art. The frequent impression in his playing of a controlled intensity, of passion contained to the very limits of the bearable, wasn't something entirely of his own doing. It had as much to do with his very being, and for some it often seemed to break the vessel that was asked to contain it. The demonic streak in Horowitz, though it declined in old age, sometimes threatened to engulf much of the music which he played. The very forcefulness of Horowitz's temperament, and its will to expression, laid him open to widespread charges of misrepresentation.

From the time of his late teens, when he had a working repertoire of over 200 pieces, Horowitz was musically omnivorous. There was virtually nothing that he didn't play in private, though his concert programmes, for the most part, continued to represent him as a virtuoso in the grand tradition. Chopin, Schumann, Scriabin and Liszt formed the core of his public repertoire, and his performances of certain twentieth-century works (most notably by Rachmaninov, Prokofiev and Barber) were near legendary. At the same time, his Scarlatti was of a quite breathtaking purity and subtlety, backed up, like most of what he played, by meticulous and scholarly research. For all his Romantic leanings, he was a painstaking stylist, capable of miraculous nuance. Yet ever since his American debut, when one critic dubbed him 'that unleashed tornado from the Steppes', Horowitz attracted audiences intent on enjoying some staggering pianistic fireworks, and he never disappointed them. His performance of the Schumann Toccata finds him very much in tornado vein, and reassuringly demonstrates that in the fever of the moment even he could hit wrong notes. He plays like a man possessed. There is a wildness that fairly defies a microphone to capture it, but even in the clinical, technologically sanitized age of digital recording you can hear why he drove people to frenzy.

In the 30 years separating Schumann's Toccata and Brahms's *Variations on a Theme of Paganini*, the piano came of age. There have been some significant developments in its evolution since 1863, but in all but a few particulars the piano Brahms wrote for was the piano we know today: its tone deeper, richer and more powerful than the pianos of Schumann's time, its action more finely honed and capable of almost infinite nuance, its massive metal frame, heavier stringing and machine-tooled hammers able to withstand unprecedented tensions. The auxiliary piano and tuner required by Liszt now belonged largely to history. In some ways, however, the Brahmsian piano with its heavier action and weightier hammers was harder to play, rendering his *Paganini Variations* a still more taxing proposition than Schumann's Toccata.

Almost a quarter-century after his death, the influence of Paganini had lost little of its inspirational power. His name remained a byword for transcendental virtuosity, and there is certainly no work of Brahms more formidable in its challenges to the pianist. Interestingly, the first variation of Book I bears a close family resemblance in its double-note figuration to the first subject of Schumann's Toccata. The

Johannes Brahms (1833–97) as a young man. Silver-point drawing by J. B. Laurens, 1853.

theme, already used by Schumann in his aforementioned *Concert Studies*, is that of Paganini's 24th *Caprice* for unaccompanied violin (given still further pianistic celebration in Rachmaninov's famous *Paganini Rhapsody* and Lutoslawski's vastly entertaining *Paganini Variations* for two pianos). Because of their obviously Étude-like character, Brahms's variations have come in for a great deal of unintentional abuse at the hands of virtuosos who appear to regard them as a kind of super-Czerny. They are, in fact, immensely resourceful and beautiful studies in pianistic tone painting, embracing not only the bravura but the lyrical and tender, and their multi-layered rhythmic textures hark back to those of Bach. There is, in fact, no other work which pays such comprehensive and inspired tribute to the piano at its coming of age, and it has had no more commanding exponent than the late Italian pianist Arturo Benedetti Michelangeli [CD 2].

Few composers have come in for more unjustified abuse when it comes to pianistic textures than Brahms, whose writing for the

Brahms at the piano.

instrument has been widely condemned by generation after generation for being 'thick', 'heavy', 'ungainly', 'stodgy', 'glutinous' and so on. The problem, more illusory than real in any case, is easily resolved if one approaches Brahms as a predominantly polyphonic composer, with his roots in Bach and such earlier masters as Schütz and Palestrina (whose music he knew intimately and often conducted). Another refreshingly different view of Brahms as a piano composer came from Artur Schnabel, who startlingly described him as 'the first Impressionist' – an illuminating commentary on the late pieces (Op. 116–19) especially. That title, however (which might with still greater justification be accorded Chopin or Liszt), is normally bestowed upon a man who wanted none of it.

Claude Debussy (1862–1918) was a born revolutionary of extraordinary refinement and minuscule generosity. Though his music often has about it a clarity and delicacy of sound which is almost Classical, he was fundamentally out of sympathy with Classical ideals of form and development. 'I am more and more convinced,' he wrote, 'that it is not in music's nature to be cast into fixed and traditional forms. It is made up of colours and of rhythms. The rest is a lot of humbug, invented by frigid imbeciles riding on the backs of the masters.' Among these 'frigid imbeciles' he was pleased to number both Mozart and Beethoven. His idol was Chopin, whose complete works he edited near the end of his life ('He was the greatest of them all, for through the piano alone he discovered everything'). Whatever his antecedents, it may fairly if a little simplistically be said that Debussy opened up an entirely new world of sound – vocal, orchestral and pianistic. To envisage the piano as 'an instrument without hammers' might on the face of it seem like idealizing the violin as 'an instrument without strings', but it gives some measure of Debussy's originality and provides a valuable key to the interpretation and understanding of his music.

If the performance of Field, Chopin and Liszt is unthinkable without the use of the pedals, the same is even truer of Debussy. There lies the secret of the piano without hammers. There lies the key to his pianistic palette, awash in a sea of symbiotic overtones. There lies the catalyst for the greatest alliance of intellect and sensuality in the history of the piano. In addition to his two magical books of Préludes, his chief piano works include the *Suite bergamasque* (source of the famous *Clair de lune*), the transfixing *Estampes* with their evoca-

Claude Debussy photographed by his wife in 1910.

tions of Spanish and oriental music, the enchanting *Children's Corner* suite, and the two books of *Images*, from the first of which comes the miraculously evocative *Reflets dans l'eau* (Reflections in the Water) [CD 2]. The late book of 12 Études, which rank in difficulty, importance and poetic vision with those of Chopin which inspired them, comes from later in Debussy's life. No. 7, *Pour les degrés chromatiques* [CD 2], is technically a study in digital dexterity but ironically requires for its full effect the impression (to extend Debussy's image) not only of a piano without hammers but of a pianist without fingers.

*   *   *

Strangely enough, with the exception of Alfred Cortot, the greatest interpreters of Debussy have not been French. Names like Sviatoslav Richter, Michelangeli, Rubinstein and Ricardo Viñes spring to mind, but the man regarded by many people as the greatest of them all was outwardly the most improbable. Walter Gieseking (1895–1956) is chiefly remembered today as one of the subtlest miniaturists in the history of pianism, yet in life he was a towering great hulk of a figure, six foot three without his shoes and tipping the scales at more than fifteen stone. And yet it fitted. The man was born with an outsize personality, and a talent to match. His self-confidence was unruffled by even the tiniest whisper of doubt. He never went to school, but

then why should he have? At the age of five he could read and write
perfectly and was gifted with apparently total recall. 'After that,' he
confessed blithely, 'I never needed to learn anything. I was, from a
tiny little chap, very fond of music and I somehow picked up piano-
playing by myself.' He made his official debut in Hanover at the age
of 20, a concert which he quickly followed up with a series of six
recitals encompassing all 32 of the Beethoven sonatas. 'The most
difficult part,' he later remarked, 'was memorizing them – and even
that wasn't very difficult.' Among his most striking characteristics was
a remarkable understanding of pianistic sonorities and a naturally
breathing style which led to an early reputation as a Chopin player.

Despite an apparently unlimited repertoire, it is with the French
impressionists that Gieseking is most famously identified. With a mind
as agile and disciplined as his fingers, and an uncanny and perhaps
unequalled virtuosity with all three pedals, he coaxed sounds from the
piano which seemed to belie its very nature. His playing of Ravel at
his Berlin debut in 1920 reduced the critics to a state of stupefied
incredulity. By common consent, his recordings of the complete
Debussy Préludes, the *Estampes* and the two books of *Images* are among
the greatest ever made.

Perhaps his favourite extra-musical activity was lepidoptery. In a
lifetime of scholarly pursuit he amassed one of the largest collections
of moths and butterflies in the world, including more than 14,000
specimens, on the basis of which he formed well-defended theories
about the early, worldwide migration of wildlife. On one occasion,
during an outdoor concert, a particularly desirable moth flew by while
Gieseking was playing. He promptly abandoned the piano in pursuit
of it and refused to continue until the moth was captured.

* * *

Such is the pairing instinct in human beings that many great composers
have been popularly yoked together like Siamese twins, often with
little more justification than contemporaneity. Thus we hear of Bach
and Handel, Mozart and Haydn, Beethoven and Schubert, Chopin

and Liszt, Bruckner and Mahler, and of course Debussy and Ravel.

Pianistically speaking, one might say that where Debussy is descended from Scarlatti, Rameau, Mozart and Chopin, Ravel belongs to the lineage of Couperin, Beethoven, Liszt and Chabrier. Certainly his style is far removed from Debussy's 'hammerless' vision of the instrument. He makes frequent use of the piano's percussive qualities, and his rhythms are generally more angular and incisive than Debussy's. His piano works show an almost obsessive preoccupation with the dance, as in the entrancing *Pavane pour une infante défunte*, the *Valses nobles et sentimentales* (its title taken straight from Schubert), and the *Forlane, Rigaudon* and *Menuet* from his best-known solo piano suite after *Gaspard de la Nuit, Le Tombeau de Couperin*.

Ravel is often and rightly thought of as a quintessentially French composer, but an important part of his own identity lay outside France. His father was Swiss and his mother was Spanish, and Spain looms large in his pianistic output, not least in his frequent use of fast repeated notes, on the model of the Spanish guitar. The most sensational of his many 'Spanish' pieces is undoubtedly the famous and finger-bleedingly virtuosic *Alborada del gracioso* from his *Miroirs* (Mirrors).

Maurice Ravel (1875–1937).

Despite their pairing in the popular imagination, it doesn't follow that a great interpreter of Debussy will be equally great in Ravel, but there are certain performers whose genius and technique appear to be all-embracing. One such was Dinu Lipatti. Unfortunately, he never recorded any Debussy, but his one recording of Ravel remains unsurpassed. For all that his life was tragically short, Lipatti remains for many connoisseurs the most profoundly satisfying pianist of the twentieth century. Born in Bucharest, Rumania, in 1917, he learned to play the piano, according to his mother, before he had even learned to smile. By the time he was four, he was already giving concerts for charity and composing. In 1934, now 17, he left Rumania and travelled to Paris where he became a pupil of Cortot (piano), Charles Munch (conducting) and Nadia Boulanger (composition), and embarked on a career far removed from the Lisztian model of manipulative showmanship. Wherever he played he occasioned not hysteria but reverence. When Francis Poulenc remarked upon Lipatti's 'divine spirituality', he spoke for many.

But there was very much more to Lipatti than 'divine spirituality'. There was a charm which was all the more endearing for being almost childlike, and when he saw fit to unleash it, a positively breathtaking virtuosity. His recording of the *Alborada del gracioso* is not only a marvel of technical control and rhythmic life but an unabashed explosion of flamboyance. It is one of the very few performances that may safely be described as definitive [CD 2]. His attitude to music was of the utmost seriousness, but he was never guilty of misplaced solemnity. He often played jazz for his own amusement, and delighted in shocking that multitude of worshippers who seemed determined to thrust sainthood on him. With his death from leukaemia at the age of 33, however, his unofficial canonization became inevitable, and there can hardly be a soul who begrudges it.

CHAPTER 7

The Maiden's Prayer

The education of women should always be relative to men. To please, to be useful to us, to make us love and esteem them, to educate us when young and to take care of us when grown up, to advise, to console us, to render our lives easy and agreeable – these are the duties of women at all times and what they should be taught in their infancy ... Women, in general, possess no artistic sensibility ... nor genius ... They can acquire a knowledge of anything through hard work. But the celestial fire that emblazens and ignites the soul, the inspiration that consumes and devours ... these sublime ecstasies that reside in the depths of the heart are always missing in women's writings. These creations are as cold and pretty as women themselves.

Jean-Jacques Rousseau, 1758

When Noël Coward, in a popular song of 1935, advised a certain Mrs Worthington not to put her daughter on the stage, he touched a perennially sensitive nerve. What to do with daughters is a question almost as old as motherhood itself. So, of course, is the matter addressed in the song – what *not* to do with them. Both questions are directly connected to class, and in all but the poorest, music has traditionally played its part in providing the answers. Only at subsistence level does the problem not arise. When physical survival is at stake, women – mothers and daughters, even the very young – bend their backs no less than men. They plough, they sow, they harvest and they procreate. As you come up the social ladder, however, all that changes. Women have time on their hands instead of calluses. Their homebound idleness has become an emblem of their husbands' prowess in the market place. Labour, except in childbirth, has become not only unnecessary but unthinkable. So what were women meant to do?

The most obvious thing – so obvious that even the most case-hardened Women's Libbers have trouble getting around it – was to become mothers, thereby perpetuating not only the species but the family name, which of course was always the man's. Before they could become mothers, however – socially acceptable mothers – they had to become wives. Or putting it another way, they had to get husbands. It was for this purpose more than any other, after all, that daughters existed. And for all but a handful of Mrs Worthingtons it was enough. A verse from the early seventeenth century puts the situation in a nutshell.

> This is all that women do:
> Sit and answer them that woo;
> Deck themselves in new attire,
> To entangle fresh desire;
> And after dinner, sing and play,
> Or, dancing, pass the time away.

Music, even in Elizabethan times, was a well-established part of any self-respecting daughter's bait. And so it continued to be, right into the early twentieth century. A hundred years earlier the science of seduction was just reaching the apex of its refinement. And it paid post-marital dividends in which husbands had a vested interest. Feminine 'accomplishments', as they were widely known, had become a major status symbol amongst the rising middle classes, enhancing the essentially ornamental role in which women of the bourgeoisie had been cast for the best part of three centuries.

Among the favourite activities for the wives and daughters of the socially ascendant were embroidery and needlepoint, whose sun has still not set, waferwork and purse netting, painting roses on buttons, the decorating of cabinet work with traceries of seaweed, filigree and varnish work, making paper ornaments, fashioning flowers out of wax or fabric, crape work, ribbon work and so on. A modicum of French and the ability to draw or paint a little, preferably in watercolours, were likewise valued, but in this 'frenzy of accomplishments', to quote one eighteenth-century commentator, music held pride of place, with the piano commanding the high ground. The goals of these endeavours were twofold. With a happy mix of ostentation and gentility, they proclaimed the affluence of those families whose wives and daughters were free of want, and more importantly, they proved an invaluable asset on the road to the altar. One need look no further than Burton's *Anatomy of Melancholy* or the novels of Jane Austen for evidence, and even in the middle of the nineteenth century little seemed to have changed. As Thackeray remarks in *Vanity Fair*:

> What causes young people to 'come out' but the noble ambition of matrimony? ... What causes them to labour at pianoforte sonatas and to learn four songs from a fashionable master at a guinea lesson ... but that they may bring down some 'desirable' young man with those killing bows and arrows of theirs?

The strategic use of music on the road to the altar was hardly confined to England. Nor was it anything new. In 1780, we find the poet Schiller undone by the playing of a comely sorceress identified only as 'Laura':

The Music Master. *Watercolour by George Goodwin Kilburne (1839–1924).*

> Oh maiden, speak! Inform this waiting ear
> Art thou in league with spirits from another sphere?
> Dissemble not, I pray, but tell me straight: Is this
> The language spoken in Elysium's bliss?

Goethe, at around the same time, was equally besotted by another keyboard strategist:

> She has a melody which she plays with the power of an angel, so simple and so soulfully. It is her favourite song and it lifts me away from all pain, confusion and caprice – even when she strikes the first note of it!

A woman who can achieve so much with the playing of a single note would seem to have no problems. Not, at least, when it comes to bagging men. But what of such accomplishments when once the ploy had worked? Robert Burton's analysis held good for the next 300 years.

> We see it daily verified in our young women and wives: They that being maids took so much pains to sing, play and dance, with such cost and charge to their parents, to get those graceful qualities, now, being married, will scarce touch an instrument. They care no longer for it.

Title page of Parthenia, *1613.*

Why, though, should women need all this artifice and guile? They have, after all, natural charms for which men have shown an insatiable appetite since the race began. And there's the nub of it. Any woman can attract a man that way. But the middle-class woman – the middle-class maiden – isn't or wasn't supposed to. She prided herself, as did her husband, on her chastity – or at least on the appearance of chastity. By making a show of it, she was able to demonstrate her moral superiority not only over the lower orders, whose wantonness was often spurred by want, but over her social betters. It was well known that women of the aristocracy used sex as a political weapon and advanced

through society horizontally. Or so the middle class liked to believe.
Small wonder, then, that for many years they adopted as the symbol
of their own gentility an instrument whose virtuous associations were
demurely proclaimed on the cover of one of the most significant
publications in keyboard history:

PARTHENIA
or The Maydenhead of the first musicke
that ever was printed for the Virginalls

The date was 1613, the collection (of works by Byrd, Gibbons and
Bull) probably the first music of any kind to have been printed from
engraved plates, and already, on its maiden voyage into print, we find
domestic keyboard music unmistakably associated with sex. Lest any
doubts remain, the collection was compiled, published and presented
to the Princess Elizabeth, daughter of King James I, on the occasion
of her marriage. However chaste the imagery, *Parthenia* (the name
itself deriving from the Greek for virgin) set the seal of royal approval
on the use of the keyboard as an agent of courtship and seduction.

Hordes of aspiring brides may have gladdened the hearts of the
clergy but they did little for the state of music. Among pupils and
teachers alike, standards had fallen like autumn leaves by the onset of
the eighteenth century. In 1750, the year of Bach's death, Friederich
Marpurg, an esteemed writer on music, published a letter purporting
to have been addressed to him by a young lady in Berlin:

> I want you to know that I think very highly of music; and not only that:
> I am having myself instructed in it with vehement ardour. I go in for the
> clavier with the greatest of pleasure and am making the most excellent
> progress. My dearest Papa got me quite a fine one at an auction and a
> rather clever suburban organist is teaching me how to play it. We have
> him come over every couple of weeks, and he gives me a half-hour lesson
> on every trip. He isn't at all expensive, and it is only about every month
> that we have to pay him 2 or 3 ducats. Every year my dear Mama
> presents him with a few pecks of oatmeal. Even if I had no natural

inclination for music, this man would be able to arouse one in me. He is very modest, and for a man of his background knows very well how to behave towards people.

And he must have been glad of the oatmeal. The finer points of his teaching methods are left to our speculation, but he evidently knew well which side of his bread got the butter:

> He always sits at my left side when I play, and he never forgets to make me a reverence from a certain English dance. He marks all the notes with letters so as not to trouble my head needlessly ... The choice of fingering, as a trifle, he leaves entirely to my own discretion. And since he is very unselfish and has no desire to hold me back, he discards all ornaments, maintaining that they only hinder speed in playing. He gives me hope that I will very soon be able to play all the latest arias. I must not forget to tell you that my cheerful master usually carries with him a mouth organ, with which he often accompanies my tones, so as to give me some idea of concertos, he says.

Not all music teachers were so enthusiastically received. More typical is the prayer which one well-born German lady remembered having said as a child: 'Dear God, Please make it so that Frau Kramer will not come today.' Frau Kramer, of course, was the piano teacher.

Herr or Doktor Kramer, too, might have been a piano teacher, and an excellent one, but he would not have been admitted to the house. The peculiarly aphrodisiac power of the piano is properly the province of the psychologist, not the musician, of course, but its existence has seldom been in doubt. For a long time, in many quarters, and in many countries, guardians of youthful virtue commonly prescribed that girls and young women should learn the piano only from teachers. of their own sex. This would ensure that they were spared the attentions of teachers like W. F. E. Bach, a grandson of Johann Sebastian's who wrote a piece for himself and two young female pupils which required all three players to sit snugly at a single piano. Naturally, he sat in the middle. Unnaturally, his own part was written to be played at the extremities of the keyboard. He called the piece

'Kisses at the Keyboard'. Illustration probably dating from the 1830s.

Das Dreyblatt, though in anticipation of one of Liszt's most famous études he might more aptly have named it *La Lecherezza.*

Liszt himself had no need of such subterfuge. His effect on the opposite sex, or to be more precise and apposite, the effect of his playing on the opposite sex, was unique in the annals of pianism. Well-born adult women threw their jewellery on to the stage, they shrieked in ecstasy (long before the bobby-soxers, teeny-boppers and groupies of the twentieth century), they fought, scratched and even kicked each other over the gloves he contrived to leave on the piano or the snuff-boxes that he just happened to have mislaid. One lady, no longer in the first flush of youth, retrieved the butt of a cigar he had smoked and sequestered it in her bosom to her dying day (in what condition one forbears to speculate).

Even when he was a wen-covered, white-haired old man in a cassock (he took minor orders in the Roman Catholic Church in 1865 and thereafter was addressed as Abbé), Liszt's effect on women was mesmeric. Such reactions as those just described were not confined, however, to women, youths and sycophants. Critics too lost all restraint, and their occasional recourse to sexual imagery was no mere chance. Consider the words of Moritz Saphir:

> Liszt is an amiable fiend who treats his mistress – the piano – now tenderly, now tyrannically, devours her with kisses, lacerates her with lustful bites, embraces her, caresses her, sulks with her, scolds her, rebukes her, grabs her by the hair, clasps her then all the more delicately, more affectionately, more passionately, more flamingly, more meltingly; exults with her to the heavens, soars with her through all the skies, and finally settles down with her in a vale of flowers covered by a canopy of stars.

Emboldened by the completion of his sentence, the poet now reloads, turning his attentions to the cost of the affair:

> After a concert, Liszt stands there like a victor on the battlefield, like a hero at a tournament. Daunted pianos lie around him; torn strings wave like flags of truce; frightened instruments flee into distant corners; the listeners look at each other as after a cataclysm of nature that has just passed by, as after a storm out of a clear sky, as after thunder and lightning, mingled with a rain of flowers and a snow of petals and a shimmering rainbow; and he stands there, leaning melancholically on his chair, smiling strangely, like an exclamation point, after the outbreak of general admiration.

We too may smile, but the evidence is overwhelming: the degree of sexuality in Liszt's aura as a performer was unprecedented, and remains unique in the history of so-called classical music. He was by no means the only virtuoso, however, who ignited the longings of his female admirers. Schumann, remember, cited another when he remarked that 'if anyone were to criticize Thalberg, all the girls in Germany, France and the other European countries would rise up in arms'. And then there was Gottschalk, too, he of the languid, dreamy eyes and invincible fingers. One gets some measure of Gottschalk's

*An 1842 impression of Liszt's
effect on female audiences.*

effect on audiences, and female audiences in particular, from the reaction of Amy Fay, a young American piano student in Europe during the 1860s, to the news of his death. 'If anything more is in the papers about him,' she wrote to a friend, 'you must send it to me, for the infatuation that I and 99,999 other American girls once felt for him still lingers in my breast.' It would be doing him an injustice, however, to suggest that such infatuations were in any way confined to the breasts of American girls. Such things acknowledge no borders.

*   *   *

The role of sex in the story of the piano is not confined to lust and the daydreams of young girls. In varying degrees, it has proved a major handicap to most women who have aspired to a performing career. The overwhelming majority of piano pupils have always been girls and young women, yet the profession of concert pianist remains even today a disproportionately male preserve. For many decades, women were largely debarred from the profession solely on account of their gender. Such things were not done by respectable girls. Felix Mendelssohn expressed the belief that his sister Fanny was even more prodigiously gifted than himself, and thoughtfully agreed to publish some of her songs under his own name, but neither he nor any of the elders in that distinguished and enlightened family would countenance the idea of her becoming a professional musician. An earlier example is Theresa Jansen, a pupil of Clementi and the daughter of a prosperous German dancing master, who was obviously a very considerable pianist indeed. One need look no further for evidence than the very difficult and brilliantly inventive sonatas that Haydn wrote for her, yet there is no evidence that she ever once played in public.

That things had changed dramatically by the middle of the nineteenth century was due to many factors, of course. European society was in ferment at almost every level. But in the story of women making music, certainly where the piano was concerned, one name stands out above all others. Clara Schumann, née Wieck, was more than the wife of a great composer and the daughter of a distinguished piano teacher. She was widely celebrated (and still is) as one of the greatest pianists of her time. Chopin said of her, 'She is the only woman in Germany who knows how to play my music properly.' She was also among the first pianists regularly to play Beethoven sonatas in public, even in Vienna, and during her many years as Robert Schumann's widow she came to be regarded (not least, it must be said, by herself) as the High Priestess of German and Germanic music. She was also a highly accomplished composer and an influential teacher. But she was not an isolated phenomenon. Other women of comparable stature though very different in character were the singer, pianist and composer Pauline Viardot (also deeply admired by Chopin), and later in the century the astonishing and equally multi-faceted Venezuelan Teresa Carreño (1853–1917), composer, brilliant virtuoso pianist and successful opera singer.

Of their predecessors, however – especially in the eighteenth century – most were disadvantaged in some way, like the blind composer–pianist Maria Theresia von Paradies, or the ugly but brilliantly gifted Josepha von Auernhammer for whom Mozart wrote his great Sonata in D for two pianos. With his customary delicacy he wrote:

> If a painter wished to portray the devil to the life, he would have to choose her face! She is as fat as a farm wench, she sweats so that you

An English family concert round the piano, c. 1840. Engraving by Alfred T. Heath after Eugene Lami.

want to vomit, and goes about so scantily clad that you can read as plain as print, 'Pray do look here.' True, there is enough to see; in fact enough to strike one blind – but one is punished for the rest of the day if one is unlucky enough to let one's eyes wander in that direction. Tartar is the only remedy, she is so horrible, so loathsome and so dirty! Augh, she is a very fright!

Mozart's horror was only intensified by the fact that he thought she planned to marry him. She herself was under no such illusion. Mozart found that out for himself when she confided in him her plan to take up music as a profession: 'I'm not pretty, I know. On the contrary, I'm very ugly. I don't care to marry some office hero with a salary of 300 gulden, and I could never get anybody different. So I'll stay as I am, and live by my talent.'

The fact is that Mozart was no Apollo himself. He was short, hook-nosed, pock-marked and cross-eyed – and if he had been judged by the same criteria as women were (and still are), he would have suffered badly for it. But he wasn't, of course. Not because he was a genius, but simply because he was a man.

Words, in the English language, are free of gender, but society seems to have decreed, not without help from women themselves, that 'plainness' is a purely feminine vice. And if Jane Austen's *Pride and Prejudice* is anything to go by, music, despite its avid cultivation by the plain, was a poor antidote. At a fashionable party in a country house, Elizabeth, the book's heroine, is persuaded to play, and even to sing, for the assembled company.

> Her performance was pleasing, though by no means capital. After a song or two, and before she could reply to the entreaties of several that she would sing again, she was eagerly succeeded at the instrument by her sister Mary, who having, in consequence of being the only plain one in the family, worked hard for knowledge and accomplishments, was always impatient for display.
>
> Mary had neither genius nor taste; and though vanity had given her application, it had given her likewise a pedantic air and conceited manner, which would have injured a higher degree of excellence than she had reached. Elizabeth, easy and unaffected, had been listened to with much more pleasure, though not playing half so well; and Mary, at the end of a long concerto, was glad to purchase praise and gratitude by Scotch and Irish airs, at the request of her younger sisters ...

Young woman playing the piano (undated illustration).

So much for knowledge and accomplishments. Scotch airs were better than serious concertos, pretty was better than plain, and that was that. But hope springs eternal, even in the plainest breast, and without it the history of music in the home would have been very different.

The example of Mary naturally had no effect whatever on the burgeoning music business. The market was there, clamouring to be wed, and music publishers on both sides of the Atlantic catered to optimistic virgins with a downpour of trifles like *The Daydream Waltz, The Last Hope,* and the *Youth, Love and Folly Polka*. By 1867, one American publisher was able to bring out a catalogue of some 360 pages, containing the titles of 33,000 pieces of music, all of them involving the piano in one way or another. They were sold individually, but when they threatened to engulf the family parlour they were gathered up and bound in leather-clad volumes which came to be known as 'Young Lady Albums'.

1860 London edition of Badarzewska's best-seller.

Just occasionally these included a sonata by Haydn or Beethoven, but far more typical of them was the century's runaway best-seller, composed by one Thekla Badarzewska (1834–61), an obscure Polish woman of microscopic talent. Strange to say, the phe-nomenal success of *The Maiden's Prayer* seems attributable solely to its title and its subsequent packaging. The piece itself is of no distinction whatever, outclassed even within its mediocre genre by literally thousands of better efforts by composers with equally undistinguished credentials. No fewer than 35 similar pieces flowed subsequently from Badarzewska's pen but none achieved any notable success. One uncharitable critic remarked in an obituary that the composer's untimely death at the age of 27 'saved the world from a veritable inundation of intolerable lachrymosity'.

Outliving her creator by many decades, the praying maiden on the cover has undergone a sequence of interesting transformations. In 1860 we find her kneeling at a prayer desk, eyes raised heavenwards, her face transfigured with contagious piety. Fifty years on, she has aged not a day but has acquired a new sophistication, and the furniture of worship has disappeared. In 1936, belying her 76 years, she appears, now standing not kneeling, in a form-hugging cocktail gown, all semblance of prayer and of maidenhood behind her. As recently as 1924, a decade after the old world order had been felled by the First

World War, a music dealer in Melbourne, Australia, sold more than 10,000 copies of *The Maiden's Prayer* in a single year. Thereafter, sales steadily declined, and the maiden was finally remaindered, though her saccharine, trivial tune still crops up from time to time in the most unexpected places. It says something interesting about the human psyche that Badarzewska's sequel, *Prayer Answered*, though in no way inferior to its antecedent, was a bust from the beginning.

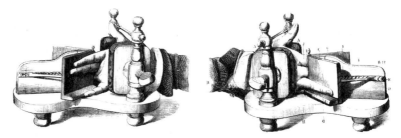

'The hand in the chiroplast'. Undated German illustration showing two views of a gadget used to strengthen pianists' hands.

CHAPTER 8
A Foot in the Door

Despite the fantasies of ivory-towered idealists, art and Mammon have seldom been strangers. Granted, music and poetry are of all arts the least material, requiring in essence no more than voice and brain for their fulfilment, but this purity exists only at a relatively low level. Instruments, from the most primitive form of percussion upwards, introduce a material element, closely followed, in most cases, by some kind of commerce: The fact is that except in its purest state, from a mother's improvised lullaby to the ritualized sophistication of Gregorian chant, music has never been a stranger to the market place, though it reached the mass market only slowly. For many years, composers and instrument makers struck a bargain with individual employers rather than the general public, but the fact remains that they were selling their wares no less than the itinerant onion vendor. The currency, however, could be unconventional. In 1707, for example, J. S. Bach, then a young man of 22, signed a contract whose like it would be difficult to find today: 'The undersigned shall henceforward be guaranteed an annual stipend of 85 gulden, 54 bushels of grain, 2 cords of wood, 2 dozen fish, and threescore faggots for kindling – to be delivered at the door in lieu of acreage.'

Composers, after all, don't live by art, or even bread, alone. There can be no doubting, however, that a conditional guarantee of bread can do wonders for the soul, and by extension for the state of art itself. Those like Bach or Haydn who enjoyed the security of enlightened patronage could generally go their own way, with a minimum of artistic compromise. Those, on the other hand, who went in for the more speculative business of selling to the general public have traditionally had a harder time of it. Mozart and Schubert, for instance, died poor for two simple reasons. They compromised too little (which is one of the reasons they were great artists), and they understood the market economy hardly at all. They knew as much about the psychology of salesmanship as most laymen know about astrophysics. Handel and Beethoven were altogether cannier. Both were prepared to write shameless pot-boilers when the need arose, and as businessmen they were appropriately unscrupulous. On the whole, however, great art and great salesmanship have not gone hand in hand. Nor are the reasons hard to find. Salesmanship, after all, consists largely in giving the public what it wants, or rather in persuading the public that it wants what you have. And since one of the commonest desires in human nature is to have something for nothing, or at any rate to extract the maximum yield from the minimum investment, great art has generally been the kiss of death for the salesman. Maria Edgeworth, writing as long ago as 1798, touched on the heart of the matter in an imaginary conversation with a fashionable lady:

> 'Would not you, as a good mother, consent to have your daughter turned into an automaton for eight hours in every day for fifteen years, for the

promise of hearing her, at the end of that time, pronounced the first private performer at the most fashionable and the most crowded concert in London?'

'For *one* concert,' says the hesitating mother, 'I think it would be too high a price. Yet I would give anything to have my daughter play better than anyone in England. What a distinction! She might get into the first circles in London! She would want neither beauty nor fortune to recommend her! She would be a match for any man who had a taste for music – and music is universally admired, even by those who have no taste for it!'

Art, in short, exacts the maximum investment of time, energy and application, and comes with no promises. In any case, for society at large, art would seem to have been the least of music's virtues. That fictitious mother may have considered 43,800 hours of her daughter's time a fair price to pay for getting into the highest circles, but how many mothers would agree? In a society where music was 'admired', even by those who had no taste for it, quality was happily sacrificed on the altar of genteel indolence. What recommended a particular song or piano piece was not its substance but its lack of difficulty. From the moment when music crept out of the confines of the court and began to be cultivated by aspiring commoners, the salesman's catchword was 'ease'. As long ago as the Elizabethan age, Thomas Morley, a great composer, issued a sophisticated treatise as 'A Plaine and Easy Introduction'. Others soon followed suit. In some cases, their claims were true, but not in most. As Shakespeare makes wickedly clear through the character of Autolycus in *The Winter's Tale*, the notorious ballad-sellers of Tudor times were quintessential con-men, who were among the first to realize that in the marketing of music, novelty ranks almost on a par with ease. If both could be combined, so much the better. No one understood this better than the so-called 'song-pluggers' of New York's aptly named Tin Pan Alley, the capital of the American popular song industry. And industry it certainly was. By the early 1900s, the sheet music revolution was in full swing, with single songs often selling as much in a year as previous hits had sold in a quarter-century. Among the 'pluggers' in 1914 was a 16-year-old named Gershwin who pounded out popular songs from dawn till dusk. Eighteen years later, now world-famous, Gershwin rebelled against the something-for-nothing brigade, with their stacks of simplified show tunes, by publishing 18 of his own biggest hit songs in a volume of piano arrangements (*George Gershwin's Songbook*) that made no concessions to the pianistic incompetents who made up the bulk of his market. A number of these arrangements are of considerable difficulty, and they add up to more keyboard fun than all the 'Young Lady Albums' of the previous century put together [CD 2].

The application of high-pressure salesmanship, however, was by no means confined to composers and middlemen. It was shared by a legion of swindlers who masqueraded under the noble name of teacher. The young Goethe, long after Autolycus had turned to dust, discovered this to his cost, as he revealed many years later in his autobiography.

> The project of having me instructed in music had long been deliberated by my parents. The final impulse to it might deserve some mention. It had already been agreed that I was to learn the clavier; there was, however, some dispute concerning the choice of a teacher. Finally I came one day by chance into the room of one of my young friends just as he was taking a lesson, and I found the teacher to be a most charming man. For each finger of the right and left hand he had a nickname, with which he designated it, in the jolliest fashion, whenever it was to be used. The black and white keys were likewise pictorially named; the very tones themselves, indeed, appeared under figurative names. The members of this colourful company were then worked into a gay interplay. Fingering and metre seemed to become quite easy and clear, and while the pupil was roused to the best of humours, everything proceeded as famously as could be.

The man's showmanship had had the desired effect, and Goethe's piano lessons began. The after-sales service, however, left much to be desired. Weeks passed with no sign of the man's former jollity. Only when a young playmate happened inadvertently to interrupt a lesson was the mystery resolved.

> All at once the pipes from the well of humour were opened: the 'thumblings' and 'pointerlings', the 'crawlers' and 'wigglers', the little

'faxies' and 'gaxies' were all at hand again and cut the most amusing capers. My young friend ... swore that he would give his parents no peace until they gave him too such an excellent man as a teacher.

'Thus, at a tender age,' Goethe ruefully concludes, 'the way to art was opened to me, according to a newer theory of education.'

Novelty again – and again the illusion of ease. They made an invincible combination. Indeed across the English Channel their alliance was menacing even the likes of Goethe's clavier instructor. In England the clavier was being usurped by another instrument. Not yet the piano, though its menace was imminent, but the guitar. And why? 'Because,' lamented the Rev. Doctor John Brown in 1758, 'the guitar is a plaything for a child; the harpsichord and the lute require application.' The short-lived fad for the guitar may not have advanced the cause of art, but as the historian Charles Burney observed, it had a stimulating effect on the musical market place.

> Its vogue was so great among all ranks of people as nearly to break all the harpsichord and spinet makers, and indeed the harpsichord teachers. All the ladies disposed of their harpsichords at auction for a third of their price, or exchanged them for guitars; until old Kirkman, the harpsichord maker, after almost ruining himself buying in his instruments, for better times, purchased likewise some cheap guitars and made a present of several to girls in milliners' shops, and to ballad singers, in the streets, whom he had taught to accompany themselves with a few chords and triplets, which soon made the Ladies ashamed of their frivolous and vulgar tastes, and return to the harpsichord.

Old Kirkman was a canny psychologist. He may have sold musical instruments, but they were bought, by and large, by unmusical customers. If he had followed the more normal line of advertising his wares on their artistic merit he would have gone to the wall. The fact that his instruments were expensive, on the other hand, greatly added to their charm. The reasons, as Maria Edgeworth observed half a century later, are perennial.

> It is the practice in high life to undervalue and avoid as much as possible everything which descends to the inferior classes of society.

'Accomplishments' have lost much of that value which they acquired from opinion since they have become common that they cannot be considered as the distinguishing characteristics of even a gentlewoman's education. The higher classes, and those who aim at distinction, now establish another species of monopoly ... They secure to themselves a certain set of expensive masters in music, drawing, dancing etc. .... They endeavour to believe, and to make others believe, that no one can be well educated without having served an apprenticeship of so many lessons under these privileged masters; they are pursued by the intrusive and vulgar. [And here she gets to the nub of it.] In a wealthy mercantile nation there is nothing which can be bought for money that will long continue to be an envied distinction.

And there, in a nutshell, is the very engine of the domestic music market. Kirkman the harpsichord maker may have won his battle with the guitar, but he was doomed to extinction by history. Harpsichords were becoming old hat; and in any case, where status symbols are concerned, society demands a rapid turnover. The guitar was just a warning. What finished Kirkman was the piano. Its advantages over the harpsichord have already been enumerated, but it had as well the virtue of being expensive, and therefore socially desirable. And the technique of playing it was similar enough to the harpsichord's so that the same teachers, and indeed the same pupils, could quickly adapt to it. Kirkman went under, but the fashionable teachers, and the charlatans with them, were riding the crest of the wave. And tumbling in their wake, upholding the timeless traditions of Autolycus and Goethe's clavier instructor, came the out and out con-men, catering as ever to the something-for-nothing brigade, and with an audacity that was little short of breathtaking.

Aiding and abetting them was a swarm of meretricious note-spinners – composers is too honourable a word – whose products were marketed with monotonous regularity, throughout the nineteenth century, as being 'brilliant but not difficult'. It was an inspired slogan, but many purchasers, on perusing these works in the comfort of their own homes, found it to have overstated the case. There was no cause for alarm. They had only to turn to that plethora of mechanical contrivances whose avowed intention was to eliminate difficulty entirely, and at no expense of effort. They did, however, require a certain expenditure of time. A case in point, the invention of one Casimir Martin, was the so-called 'Chirogymnaste', extolled as follows in the pages of the Parisian *Gazette Musicale*:

> If one had the patience to study with the 'Chirogymnaste' for three or four years, one could be a great pianist without ever having placed one's fingers on the keyboard. The 'Chirogymnaste' has another immense advantage, that of being entirely silent – of educating the hand and the fingers without ever tiring the ear. The 'Chirogymnaste' could only be rejected by those people who find that pianists are already too numerous and who consequently must condemn an apparatus that will multiply them still further, since it cuts down by at least two thirds the study time that the piano requires today.

Aspiring virtuosos to whom even that one remaining third seemed an intolerable price to pay for greatness could forestall despair by turning to an invention of the fashionable salon pianist Henri Herz. Trendily dubbed the 'Dactylion' (a Greek-sounding name was ever a winning sales ploy), this impressive device relied on ten vertical springs suspended over the keyboard and terminating in ten rings, one for each finger. The strain on the spring when you depressed a key was designed to encourage a quick lifting of the fingers, thereby ensuring a miraculous improvement in your keyboard articulation. And Herz provided an exemplary after-sales service. For those uncertain of how to proceed, once trussed up, he published a companion volume of a thousand exercises.

Herz may have ranked high, but the uncrowned king of the shysters was J. B. Logier, best remembered today for his invention of the 'Chiroplast', a mechanical swindle of unparalleled audacity which enjoyed a surprisingly widespread vogue in the early 1800s. It came in four sections, best described, perhaps, in the sales brochure compiled by the inventor himself. First came the 'Gamut Panel':

> an oblong board, which on one side has drawn upon it two staves of five lines each, one for the treble, the other for the bass, containing all the

notes used in music, so written that when placed over the keys of a piano, each note, with its name, will be exactly over its corresponding key.

Next comes the 'Position Frame', which consists of two parallel rails, extending from one extremity of the keyboard to the other; to the two ends of these are fixed two cheek pieces, which by means of a brass rod and extending screw are attached firmly to the instrument. The rails may be adjusted by means of screws in the cheek pieces, so as to admit the hands of the pupil passing between them, nearly as far as the wrists, and being so regulated as to prevent any perpendicular motion of the hands.

The 'Finger Guides' consist of two moveable brass plates with five divisions through which the thumb and four fingers are introduced. These divisions correspond perpendicularly with the keys and may be moved to any situation by means of the brass rod on which they are made to slide.

There remains but the 'Wrist Guide', this being a brass wire, with a regulator attached to each finger guide, to prevent the wrists from being inclined outwards.

Strange to relate, the inventor made a small fortune from the sales of his infernal device, submission to which enjoyed a considerable vogue on both sides of the Atlantic, thanks in part to the surprising number of endorsements from famous artists, among them the redoubtable Muzio Clementi, who wrote earnestly, 'I have examined this new invention, called the Patent Chiroplast, and am so well persuaded of its great utility that I cannot but give it the warmest approbation and recommendation.' By the time he wrote this, Clementi had retired from the concert platform to become a successful publisher, piano manufacturer and entrepreneur. His avowed enthusiasm for the Chiroplast is best explained, perhaps, by a small notice at the end of Logier's own brochure. 'This apparatus,' it reads, though in small print, 'is manufactured by Messrs.

Logier's Chiroplast, 1819.

An advertisement for Weber pianos in the 1870s.

Clementi & Company, Cheapside, London, and may be had of all the principal Music Sellers in the United Kingdom. Price, with Instruction Book, 5 guineas.'

* * *

The rapid-fire rise in the popularity of the piano can be traced by even a cursory glance at the sales records of its makers. In 1827, for instance, Pleyel of Paris employed roughly 30 men and produced an average of 100 pianos a year. Within less than a decade, the work force had risen to 250 and the annual output to nearly 1,000 – an increase of 900 per cent. Nor was this anything like an isolated phenomenon. With the spectre of supply outstripping demand hovering ever above their shoulders, the manufacturers grew increasingly dependent on successful marketing. And the competition was fearsome. In one memorable encounter in the corridors of a Philadelphia hotel, the piano-movers of two rival makes met in battle, using as weapons the unscrewed legs of their respective instruments. Remarkably, there were no fatalities. But in the market outside the stakes were high, and the salesmen were run ragged. Their approaches were several, but beneath the fancy language of the advertising men the principles of the salesmen were broadly speaking much the same.

In America, particularly, quantity was easily, if not habitually, confused with quality. In the 1870s, potential buyers were inundated with sales and manufacturing statistics as though popularity was synonymous with value. One make bureaucratically announced that 'The sale of Weber pianofortes has increased in four years by 368 per cent, as per Internal Revenue returns, while the other leading Pianoforte Houses have increased by only 20 to 25 per cent.' Haines countered by proclaiming themselves 'The largest manufacturers of square pianos in the U.S.', and boasted, by way of proof, that they were 'now producing forty pianos per week'. Steinway's were unimpressed. They, after all, were producing 'One new piano every working hour! Ten pianos every day!' Chickering, taking a longer perspective, modestly revealed in 1873 that 'Forty-one thousand

Chickering and Sons' advertisement, 1873.

Chickering pianofortes have been made and sold since 1823!' Work it out by the week, and it comes to a mere 15, lagging behind Haines' weekly output by fully 25, and leaving Steinway's with a commanding lead – 50 pianos per week (their annual output being 2,600).

It must not be thought, however, that an obsession with large numbers is a purely American phenomenon. In Britain, too, both public and press were subject to fits of advanced numeritis, and the soaring popularity of the piano reflected in part its status as a wonder of industrial technology. One writer eagerly informed his readers that the action for a single Broadwood piano boasted no fewer than '3,800 separate pieces of ivory, woods, metals, cloth, felt, leather and vellum', while another marvelled that 'a grand piano passes under the hands of upwards of forty different workmen'.

Among the most successful (and sometimes the most expensive) sales ploys is the suggestion of quality through association, a system of tacit endorsement which is most conspicuously applied today in the realm of sports and athletics. The practice of paying a commission to famous musicians for lending their names to the sale of a particular make was already in full swing by the end of the eighteenth century, not least in Vienna, a city of relatively modest size which harboured a record number of pianists and piano teachers and no fewer than ten rival manufacturers. Beethoven was besieged with offers of complimentary pianos in exchange for his endorsement, and not by Austrian makers alone. Among his favourite pianos was an instrument shipped to him at enormous expense, of money and effort alike, by John Broadwood of London. Nor was Beethoven alone. Erard of Paris, quite unsolicited, sent complimentary pianos not only to Beethoven but to Haydn and the then highly esteemed but now largely forgotten Leopold Koželuh, but not before doing the same for Napoleon Bonaparte. The practice continues to this

The Steinway factory from 1854 to 1860.

day, with many a famous pianist tied to a particular make in the same way that pubs are tied to particular brewers – 'Sviatoslav Richter plays only the Yamaha', 'Evgeny Kissin plays only a Steinway' and so on.

No make, however, could compete in testimonials with Steinway, whose roster has always read like a *Who's Who* of pianists. The cost of this practice, however, could be higher than anticipated. Paderewski, a Steinway artist, discovered this at first hand while on a tour of Russia.

> When I arrived at the hall, half an hour before the concert, I found to my horror that one of the pedals of the instrument had been completely destroyed. It had clearly been ripped off with great violence; and when I tried the piano I found, between many of the keys, sharp pins standing up. I saw them, thank God, before touching the piano. And the reason for this persecution? Simply that I hadn't applied to the local piano agency in St Petersburg but had brought my own instrument instead.

In 1893, Paderewski was scheduled to play at the great World's Fair in Chicago. For various reasons, among them a chauvinistic determination on the part of the fair's organizers to favour Chicago's own industries against all interlopers, Steinway decided that in this case they would give the fair a miss. Theodore Thomas, America's leading conductor and a prime mover behind the musical activities at the fair, was approached by a posse of local piano manufacturers demanding from him a guarantee that no piano by a non-exhibiting maker would be played at the fair. Four days before Paderewski's scheduled appearance, notice was given that 'if any Steinway pianos are announced for concerts at the Exposition grounds, the Director General is authorized to send in teams to dump the pianos outside the gates'. Further, it was stated that 'the bills announcing Mr Paderewski's appearance will be taken down, and Mr Paderewski's name erased'. In the event, Paderewski did play his concert, on a Steinway that had been smuggled in under the name of 'hardware'. The concert was a sensation, no team of heavies arrived to besmirch the atmosphere, and Paderewski's piano remained undisturbed. The local press, however, engaged in a frenzy of mud-slinging, accusing the great Pole of displaying contempt for the United States, and Thomas of being 'a small despot', 'a dull, opinionated man', 'a pragmatic curmudgeon', and opining further that he 'should have been the leader of a barrack band in a mountainous camp in North Germany'. The final upshot of all this was a degree of publicity for Steinway such as they could barely have hoped to achieve had they exhibited.

At the bottom end of the market, competition was, if anything, still fiercer, with ethics high on the list of casualties. Perhaps the most shameless and cynical of all pianistic sales ploys was the great stencil racket: the widespread application, principally in America, of a simple ruse by means of which inferior instruments, often little better than high-class junk, had stencilled on their fallboards the names of fake piano makers calculated to sound like real ones: Steinmay or Stemway, for instance, instead of Steinway, Bachstein instead of Bechstein, Pickering instead of Chickering and so on. The arch-perpetrator of this (amazingly enough, legal) technique was a New England businessman, one Joseph P. Hale, who knew as much about music and pianos as the Statue of Liberty. Such was the fashion for the piano that he reasoned, quite rightly, that many, perhaps even most of his potential customers knew even less about pianos than he did. If it had the right appearance, if it had keys activating hammers activating strings, it was a piano. What did his dupes know of the myriad refinements that separated genuine Steinways from Steinmays?

Another ploy was to blind the buyer with technology and a meaningless, grandiloquent vocabulary. One maker offered 'a semi-grand on the principle of the speaking trumpet', perhaps hoping to upstage another whose instruments claimed to be 'backed on the principle of the violoncello'. And what was one to make of a 'Registered Tavola Pianoforte' in which 'a drawing room table stands upon the centre block or pedestal and contains a pianoforte (opening with spring bolts) on the Grand principle'? The clincher here would seem to have been the inclusion of an irresistible extra, namely 'a closet containing music composed by the inventor'.

Elsewhere the bemused shopper was assailed by a range of instruments variously labelled 'Michrochordan', 'Acrosonic', 'Console', 'Harmomelo', 'Registered Compensation', 'Lyra Cottage', 'Microphonic', 'Utiliton', 'Vertichord' and many other similar and equally

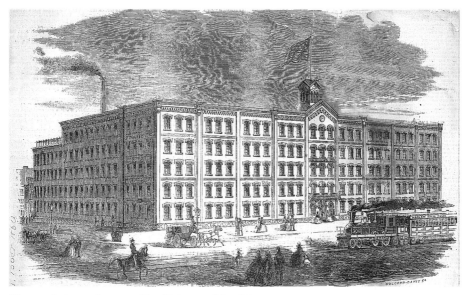

The new Steinway factory in New York, opened in 1860.

A Chappell 'pianino', or miniature piano.

empty names. One maker offered his interesting 'compressed pianofortes', another a politically correct 'Piano for the People', while Mr J. H. R. Mott of London was pleased to announce his 'Patent, Everstanding [!] and *Ne Plus Ultra* Pianos', clearly not intended for the same market as another maker's 'Artisan Piano', meekly sporting a truncated compass and plain wooden keys. One Harrison's 'Piccolo Utilitarian Boudoir Pianoforte' economized on strings, having only one per note in place of the usual three. Minimalism was not born yesterday: other popular pianistic midgets included 'Pianettes', 'Boudoir Cottages', 'Piccolos', 'Pianinos' – and one maker was publicly congratulated on his 'little Quaker-like pianos', offered to 'the public of small means – the needy clerk, the poor teacher, the upper class mechanic'.

One of the strangest episodes in the marketing of pianos occurred in America in the last quarter of the nineteenth century. In the aftermath of the Civil War, an unlikely alliance was formed between the makers of pianos and the manufacturers of sewing machines. Both were products widely used by women at home, both were widely seen as triumphs of American engineering and industrial enterprise, and both could be had for a roughly similar price. The G. E. Van Syckle Co. of Bay City, Michigan, manufactured both, and itinerant sales representatives in far-flung rural districts frequently carried both in their wagons. Further east, a firm in Connecticut, spotting a hole in the market, made a combination sewing machine and melodeon. There was even a publication, launched in 1880, entitled the *Musical and Sewing Machine Gazette*. But all good things must come to an end. After only nine issues, the journal folded and was reborn as the *Musical Courier*, with nary a sewing machine in sight.

The showroom of the piano firm Blüthner in Leipzig, 1887.

CHAPTER 9

An Invincible Alliance

At the opposite pole to the cosy, convivial domestic repertoire of the eighteenth and nineteenth centuries lies the fantasy of every aspiring pianist: the big, Romantic, virtuoso concerto, in which dashing pianistic Davids triumph over an army of orchestral Goliaths (never mind that the dice are loaded). In no medium is the symbolic character of the modern concert grand more vividly, more lavishly realized. In the concerto, as nowhere else, the eternal conflicts between individual liberty and the communal good are played out again and again. Interestingly, however, the keyboard concerto was a relatively late arrival on the European stage. The concerto idea, on the other hand, based on the alternation or opposition of contrasting forces (the few, or the one, as against the many), is almost as old as music itself. In the history of Western art, it goes back at least to the days of the ancient Greeks, and finds later antecedents in the Shakespearian soliloquy and the early operatic aria, but its roots are prehistoric, and may at least be glimpsed in the music of tribes whose way of life has remained essentially unchanged for many thousands of years. In every society, from the most primitive to our own, music has played a symbolic role, in which the relationship of the one to the many, of the individual to the community, has played a major part. Indeed that relationship has been central to the survival of music itself, from the most primeval ritual to the piano concertos of J. C. Bach and Elliott Carter. As the nature of that symbolism is common to both, it might be useful, from a sociological point of view, to approach the latter by way of the former.

In the cultures of present-day primitives, no less than in the hi-tech world of digital recording, songs, while obviously originating with an individual, stand or fall on the basis of community approval. In many tribes, the acceptance or rejection of songs isn't left to chance and time, but put to the test at formalized rituals akin to the modern auction. In illiterate societies, music survives only with communal approbation. The Romantic Western notion of the inspired artist, working away at his masterworks in a garret, is a child of affluence. In early or archaic societies, music belongs to everyone or no one.

The powerfully cohesive nature of music in primitive cultures is evident in the prevalence of collective performance. Not only funeral music (which one might expect) but even love songs are predominantly choral. So close, indeed, is the relationship between the individual and society that newly-weds are often serenaded throughout their wedding night by the community at large. This isn't to say, however, that distinctions between the one and the many don't exist. In music, as in the wider spheres of tribal life, the leaders are clearly distinguished from the led. In the near-universal use of the 'call and response' technique, for instance ('responsorial singing' to musical initiates), the leader tends to perform in a sharp and rather abrupt style, while the chorus will answer with a more song-like, caressing approach. Such contrasts are the bread and butter of musical form, and nowhere more so than in the instrumental concerto. Music, even at the lowest level, is fundamentally opposed to anarchy. Where we find music, we find order. And in the nature of that order, nine times out of ten, we find a kind of Utopian blueprint, albeit very basic, of the society to which it speaks.

This innate sense of order, informed by the relentless duality of a two-legged, two-armed, two-eyed, two-eared, two-sexed race, is reflected even in the lowest forms of musical culture. In the palaeolithic tribes in the jungles of the Amazon or the rain forests of Sri Lanka, as in numerous less primitive societies the world over, two clear-cut and opposing styles flourish side by side. The first casts music as a vehicle for the magic of words (as in the operatic aria of our own culture, whose relevance to the concerto, as we shall see, is fundamental). Characterized by a monotony incomprehensible to civilized ears, it alternates between a mere two notes, one invariably emerging as central, the other representing a diversion. It is a principle that lies at the very heart of all so-called tonal music and reaches its apotheosis in the Classical era dominated by Haydn, Mozart and Beethoven. The second style gives vent to passion, the voice leaping to a great height and tumbling down in long, wailing cataracts of sound, with little semblance of order between the highest and lowest notes, which themselves remain constant. In this style, the two fixed pitches conform to a single universal standard known in Western jargon as the octave (and comparable here to what we call the 'tonic'). This boundary, indeed, dominates the whole of humanity's music, whatever its age, type or provenance, up to, and including, the atonal revolutions of the twentieth century.

Whatever its range of styles and formal purposes, music reflects a variety of needs and tendencies which are common to us all and which find their natural expression in the language of metaphor. Among these is a sense of community combined with a fundamental if ambivalent desire for leadership. Which brings us back to the 'call and response' technique in which a soloist–leader is answered by a chorus (the forerunner of our orchestra), whose corporate repetitions enhance the authority of the idea being expressed, be it musical, symbolic, predominantly practical, or all three together, as in work songs. From the Kalahari Desert and the Serengeti Plain to the Vatican City, the streets of New Orleans and Carnegie Hall, this responsorial technique has dominated musical textures through more centuries than we can count, and reaches its instrumental peak in the piano concertos of Mozart and Beethoven. Quite apart from its social ramifications, its purely musical properties illustrate in the simplest form what may well be the single most fundamental principle of composition, certainly in the West and probably in the world: that of variation. In the alternation of soloist and choir, each singing the same material, we overcome, at least for a while, the potentially enervating effects of repetition by the simple expedient of varying the texture. And varied repetition is of fundamental importance to the classical notion of so-called 'sonata form', which underpins virtually every piano concerto from J. C. Bach to Shostakovich. At one level, the concerto may even be seen as a barometer of the changing, as well as the eternal, relationship of the individual to society, be it a monarchy, republic, dictatorship, commune, or even the extended family.

* * *

The keyboard has played a part in the story of the concerto from the beginning, but until Bach promoted it to the rank of soloist in the Fifth Brandenburg Concerto (where it shares the honours with flute and violin and has the limelight entirely to itself in a long, magnificent and quite unprecedented solo cadenza), the harpsichord, like musicians themselves, indeed like the vast bulk of the population prior to the mid-eighteenth century, played an important but servile role as a strictly supplementary part of the band as a whole.

Having liberated the harpsichord in the Fifth Brandenburg, Bach used it repeatedly as the solo instrument in concertos, and these keyboard concertos (including ones for two, three and even four harpsichords and strings) are still often played on the piano, despite the vogue for 'authenticity' which looked for a time like swamping the

1744 engraving of a concerto for keyboard, strings and wind.

musical world in the last quarter of the twentieth century. These works are a far cry from the virtuoso showpieces of the nineteenth century. The keyboard is presented as a kind of 'first among equals', although it would be idle to pretend that the virtuoso element is missing altogether. Like the Fifth Brandenburg, the famous D minor Concerto is fraught with difficulties for the soloist, and there is no attempt to conceal them from the audience, but there are only occasional instances of the spotlit soliloquizing later to become such a hallmark of the breed. Bach's emancipation of the keyboard accurately, though probably unintentionally, reflected the changes transforming society at large. And thereby hangs a tale, for which it will be necessary to backtrack a little.

The use of a keyboard instrument as a standard part of the Baroque orchestra arose largely from a need to supplement the often anaemic tone of the stringed instruments and to provide a harmonic, essentially chordal backdrop to the intertwinings of the contrapuntal weave above. It also served to provide a precise rhythmic framework, marking the beginnings of beats rather in the nature of a supermusical metronome. The term *continuo* for this part is more or less self-explanatory, deriving from the simple fact that while other instruments may drop out and re-enter, the keyboard accompaniment continues throughout (an alternative name for the same procedure is 'thorough bass', a corruption of 'through bass', i.e. a bass which continues or goes 'through' the whole composition).

Throughout the Baroque era it was customary to write out only the bass line of these keyboard accompaniments, and to indicate the required harmonies by means of various Arabic and Roman figures, leaving the means of their fulfilment to the discretion of the player, who could respond with anything from simple block chords to considerable elaboration. The ability to do this required a very thorough knowledge of both harmony and counterpoint, the latter being especially important in comparatively thin or exposed textures, in which the keyboard must avoid duplication of the melodies written out by the composer for the other instruments. A keyboard player's reputation often rested as much on the ability to do this as on the performance of fully notated solo works.*

With the rise of a mercantile middle class in the eighteenth century, this learned, sophisticated art fell increasingly by the wayside, as the long reign of polyphony gave way to the simpler textures of accompanied melody, known as 'monody'. The decline in power of the ruling aristocracy and the upward social mobility of the emerging bourgeoisie brought about radical change in 'enlightened' taste. Nowhere is this more stridently articulated than in the writings of Jean-Jacques Rousseau, philosopher and self-styled composer, whose influence was out of all proportion to the quality of his thought. Shortly after the death of Bach, Rousseau came out with a blistering attack on everything that Bach and his age had stood for.

---

*Readers wishing to pursue a hands-on approach to this technique can profitably turn to the four pages which Bach devotes to it in the musical 'notebook' compiled for his second wife, Anna Magdalena.

Fugues, imitations, double designs, and all complex contrapuntal structures ... these are arbitrary and purely conventional devices which have hardly any merit save that of a difficulty overcome – difficult sillinesses which the ear cannot endure and reason cannot justify. They are evidently the remains of barbarism and bad taste, that only persist, like the portals of our Gothic churches, to the shame of those who have had the patience to construct them. [*Lettre sur la Musique Française*, 1753]

Rousseau's spleen-venting, however, was not confined to music. He advocated in all things a 'natural simplicity', arguing that man in his natural state was essentially virtuous while the rest of humanity had been corrupted by the artifice of civilization. Redemption was possible only by a return to the values of 'natural man'. The concept of 'the noble savage' held an extraordinary appeal for mid-eighteenth-century Europeans, though not one in a thousand had the slightest inkling of the musical bonds discussed above.

Rousseau's writings were enormously influential (indeed, at the most serious level they led straight to the French Revolution). There was scarcely a genteel home that didn't suffer at least a mild attack of creeping Rousseauism, and the virus was a stranger to national boundaries. In Germany and Austria, no less than in France, the great man's writings were highly esteemed by the burgher class, and composers, even great ones, took to dressing up country-dances, or inventing spurious ones of their own. The fashion for folkiness as a musical spice had once been confined to a few isolated outbreaks, but from the middle of the eighteenth century until well into the nineteenth it acquired the status of an epidemic, bespeaking, at one level, a simpleness of mind and a weakness for stereotypes to which the standard virtuoso concerto of the nineteenth century pandered without shame. In these grandiose, simplistic dramas, which proliferated like the proverbial rabbits, the concert hall might be said to have anticipated the Hollywood Western by roughly a century. Here, in the stark opposition of good and bad, large and small, heroic and tender, Rousseau's musical chickens came back to roost. Except in their style and sophistication of means, these corrupt gladiatorial combats were not so very different in kind from the primitive call-and-response rituals of the stone-age warrior. Viewed from this perspective, the brief but golden age of the Classical concerto can all too easily be perceived as a false dawn. The journey from innocence to decadence was accomplished with unseemly haste.

* * *

The story of the authentic piano concerto really begins with Mozart, unless one includes the many agreeable concertos of J. C. Bach – the first man ever to play a piano concerto in public. Most of these, however, work just as well on the harpsichord. Mozart's 'mature' concertos,

A ticket for one of the concerts given by J. C. Bach and Abel in London between 1764 and 1781.

on the other hand, were not only composed specifically for the piano, but so idiomatically that they are scarcely conceivable on any other instrument. They also bring the piano concerto to a peak of perfection. There were subsequent developments in the medium, of course – nobody is about to discount the concertos of Beethoven, Schumann or Brahms – but Mozart's, by common consent, remain unsurpassed and seldom equalled (surprisingly, Haydn's concertos show none of the inspiration that permeates his symphonies and string quartets).

The concerto as Mozart first encountered it was an inheritance from the High Baroque, where it was unchallenged as the most popular form of instrumental music. During the first half of the eighteenth century, however, it gradually ceded pride of place to the newly developing symphony, without absorbing much of its influences. Whereas the guiding principle of the symphony was that of thematic development, the concerto clung to the standardized and somewhat static nature of its Baroque forebears. Its straightforward structure and its scope for repetition, varied only or principally by contrasts of instrumental texture, made it a natural favourite with composers and listeners of limited imagination, of whom there were a steadily increasing number. Among the best was Johann Christian Bach, whose many offerings, for all their principled superficiality, retain their elegance and charm to this day. No two are quite identical in structure, but as a whole they conform to a fairly stereotyped pattern, adopted by many lesser talents.

Of the standard three movements (fast–slow–fast), the first generally consists of an opening orchestral section in the home key, followed by a solo discourse on the same material, also in the home key. The orchestra, in an abbreviated form of the opening, now modulates to a closely related key, usually the dominant, in which the first large-scale section, the exposition, comes to a close. The central development section is generally dominated by the soloist, the orchestra being reduced to little better than an accompanying lackey. Only after this is the orchestra allowed a return to the foreground for the beginning of the recapitulation. By and large, this consists of a slim-line version of the exposition, giving way to a solo cadenza (traditionally improvised) before a final return to the opening material for a formal close.

The second movement often follows a similar procedure, though in contrasting mood, key and tempo: slow, but not too slow, essentially lyrical, though with greater harmonic and structural freedom than in the first movement, and still weighted heavily in favour of the soloist. The finale, by contrast, is generally virtuosic and quick, though some composers were happy to close with a graceful dance in the style of an extended minuet. The guiding principle, a clear offshoot from the operatic aria, is that of melody (solo) and accompaniment (orchestra). This, then, was the concerto as Mozart inherited it: essentially a lightweight vehicle for instrumental virtuosity in which foppish good manners and an unassuming tunefulness prevailed over emotional depth or meaningful dialogue.

For all their ease of access, these elegant exercises in mid-century *galanterie*, with their straightforward melody-and-accompaniment approach, continued to reflect a stratified society in which a wealthy aristocracy (as symbolized by the soloist) held sway over the far more numerous populace of its subordinates (the acquiescent orchestra). It seems singularly appropriate that it was Mozart, the first great composer to exchange the shackles of patronage for the life of the freelance, who first enabled orchestra and soloist to engage in continuous conversation at the highest level. Both the level and the nature of the dialogue in Mozart's mature concertos were unprecedented, as was his promotion of the wind section to the front ranks of musical diplomacy. From 1777 onwards, bar a few optional exceptions, Mozart gives the wind band a dual role: as a magical blending agent in his orchestral palette, and as a mediator between the soloist and the rest of the orchestra. In Mozart, for the first time, we sometimes find the soloist actually accompanying the orchestra. The dialogue between oboe and piano in the opening Allegro of the wonderful E flat Concerto, K271 [CD 3] was the first of many such charming exchanges. The integration of the one among the many, the combining of parts into a greater whole, were some of Mozart's most far-reaching achievements.

It was in 1773, at the age of 17, that he composed his first purely original concerto (the D major, K175), by which time he was already a veteran of the musical theatre, with three tours of Italy and six original operas behind him – and it showed. Nowhere in Mozart's concertos are operatic principles, or operatic procedures, very far from the surface. Indeed the whole of the extraordinary, almost uniquely profound slow movement of K271 can be seen as one great instrumental operatic *scena*. At the same time, Mozart lifted the concerto to previously unimagined heights and was the first to give it equal status with the symphony. Significantly, from a social point of view, this early D major Concerto marked the first of many occasions on which Mozart was well ahead of his audiences. Its contrapuntal finale struck his contemporaries as excessively severe (a finale that demanded concentration was one innovation too many). Mozart therefore gave it an alternate finale, now best known as the self-contained Rondo in D, K382 – a parade of unchallenging delights which guaranteed its immediate and overwhelming success. Two more delightful concertos followed, and then came one that lifted the form onto another plane altogether.

Extract from Mozart's written out Cadenza for his Piano Concerto no. 9 in E flat, K271, published by Offenbach in 1804.

With its stunning originality and its unprecedented emotional range, the E flat Concerto of 1777, K271, marks perhaps the greatest watershed in the whole history of the form. Its second bar alone must have snapped its first audience to attention like an electric shock. Immediately after the opening six-note fanfare, the soloist enters, breaking with the practice of every concerto up to that time and completing the opening idea unaccompanied. After a brief, good-natured tug-of-war, the piano retreats while the orchestra gets on with the business of the 'real' exposition. When the piano re-enters the fray, it again parts company with tradition by coming in several bars early with a long tension-building trill. From the beginning, and for the first time in the history of the medium, soloist and orchestra appear as equal partners in a genuine dialogue which continues throughout the concerto. A further departure from the norm is the insertion of what amounts to a second slow movement in the middle of the finale.

With only a couple of exceptions, every one of Mozart's subsequent concertos is a work of the highest art. And while no two are quite alike in design (generally a hallmark of the great composer), they do, of course, have many features in common. Among these is an opening orchestral exposition of the main themes, which unlike the normal exposition in an instrumental sonata remains in the home key (tonic). The piano then enters, either with the first main theme or with an entirely new (but related) idea, as in Nos. 21 and 25, and both minor-key concertos (Nos. 20 and 24).

The principal material is then explored in generally conversational style by both soloist and orchestra. In this section the piano usually indulges in some purely pianistic figuration by way of establishing its own distinct individuality and introducing a clearly competitive element. In this radically more varied approach to the material and shape of the opening, orchestral exposition, the tension of opposing keys and the alternation of stability and flux play a crucial part, as in the solo sonata, and the first big 'solo' section ends with a firm cadence in the secondary key (the 'dominant' in the case of major-key concertos, the 'relative major' in minor-key concertos).

The central development tends to follow the usual procedures, drifting through several keys, and exploring new aspects of the relationship between solo and orchestra. Before the end of the third main section, the recapitulation, the orchestra always comes to a dramatically inconclusive stop (technically a 6/4 chord) and the piano then leaps into the breach and plays around with the various themes in a highly brilliant and improvisatory way (it was expected at the time that this cadenza should indeed be improvised on the spot) before welcoming the orchestra back with a long trill, after which a (generally brief) coda – shared, in the case of No. 24 – brings the first movement to a close.

As in solo sonatas, the slow middle movement (often not so slow, in Mozart's case) is likely to be cast either as a 'sonata form' or as a 'theme and variations' (Nos. 15 and 18); and the finale is usually a rondo, but may also be another 'sonata form' movement or a set of variations.

It fell to Mozart to win for the concerto the same degree of structural and emotional mastery that Haydn had won for the symphony. The concerto as he left it, and the piano concerto in particular, was transformed almost beyond recognition. In place of the stereotyped virtuoso vehicle and the facile conversation piece cultivated by even the best composers of his youth, Mozart left a form in which the subtlest tonal variety played a prime part in the formal, colouristic

Jullien conducting in the English Opera House in 1843.

and expressive cohesion of large-scale structures; a miraculous and paradoxical tapestry of interweaving strands in which unity was achieved through continuous diversity; an instrumental drama as eloquent and various as any opera – and above all, a Utopian vision of a world without victors and vanquished, a 'republic of equals', to borrow a phrase from Schumann, in which altruism and self-interest are so intimately linked that they become indistinguishable.

The Classical concerto reached its climax with Beethoven, who also forged the key to the Romantic concerto of the nineteenth century. The first two of his seven concertos with piano* are clearly inspired by Mozartian models, but already one can sense the developments to come. Among Beethoven's major innovations was the increased importance of the orchestra, to the extent that his last two, despite their three-movement layout, can almost be perceived as symphonies with piano *obbligato*. He was also the first composer to link movements together without a break (specifically, the middle and last movements of his Fourth and Fifth Concertos) – an idea later borrowed by Mendelssohn and Schumann and further developed by Liszt.

If Beethoven's first two concertos can be seen as further developments of the Mozartian model, the Third, in C minor, introduces us to a new figure in the history of the form, and again it mirrors developments in the outside world. Here we get our first glimpse of the Romantic hero in the concerto, the glorious (sometimes vainglorious) individual who dares to stand apart from society and hurl thunderbolts at conventional assumptions. This is the Beethoven who five years later, in the famous Fifth Symphony, will 'take Fate by the throat' (his phrase).

In his Fourth Concerto he goes the Mozart of K271 one better by beginning the work with a short piano solo, which the orchestra then answers with one of the most magical key changes ever conceived. And in the Fifth (known in English-speaking countries as the 'Emperor') he allows the orchestra a single introductory chord before the soloist

---

* The five solo concertos, the Triple Concerto (for piano, violin and cello) and the piano arrangement of the Violin Concerto.

grandiloquently enters with a long, brilliant and resplendent cadenza, enhanced by two widely separated chords of support from the orchestra. With the piano's heroic credentials firmly established, the orchestra then takes over with an exposition of extraordinary grandeur. Another innovation is the built-in cadenza, with the specific instruction 'do not make a cadenza here but go on at once to the following'. And this, in turn, breaks new ground by allowing the orchestra to accompany the soloist from bar 19 of the cadenza onwards.* For all the heroics of the solo part, this is no Romantic ego-trip but one of Beethoven's most tightly 'organic' works, yet the prevailing feeling is expansive rather than compressed.

With Beethoven, too, the extemporized cadenza became largely a thing of the past. Among those who followed his example, incorporating the cadenza into the main body of the movement, were Mendelssohn, Schumann, Brahms and Tchaikovsky.

Taking his cue from Beethoven, Liszt, in his two concertos, further developed the idea of connecting movements, not just by composing links between them but by means of shared thematic material, running through the whole work in each case but modified in rhythm, tempo and mood to suit the prevailing character of each movement individually. As he was to do still more ingeniously in his great B minor Sonata some years later, he created what was in effect a single, unified structure, whose apparently self-defined movements served on a higher level of coherence as exposition, development and modified recapitulation.

However disciplined and inventive Liszt was in unifying large-scale structures, he remained in his concertos (especially in the first) a gladiatorial virtuoso who was perhaps too ready to put bravura display before expressive or dramatic substance. This was, in fact, to become the principal hallmark of the Romantic concerto: a shamelessly rigged

---

*A further development of this idea occurs in the cadenza of Beethoven's own curiously slapdash arrangement for piano and orchestra of his great Violin Concerto in D. In the piano version the soloist is accompanied through much of the cadenza by the timpani, whose four unaccompanied strokes introduce the first movement and provide much of the basis for its subsequent development.

encounter between a heroic soloist and a wing-clipped orchestra, whose main function was to glorify the pianist with a lot of empty sabre-rattling or meek accompaniments. In certain cases the organization of the music itself was of sufficient interest to compensate for the dice-loading, as in the case of the Liszt E flat [CD 3]. This much (and often unfairly) abused work had its first performance in 1855, with Liszt himself as soloist and Berlioz as conductor. Yet the original sketches for it date from 1830, a full quarter-century earlier. Whatever may be said of it – and one critic has proclaimed it 'the most vulgar concerto ever written' – the work is of historical importance, being, in the words of Béla Bartók (no vulgarian he), 'the first perfect realization of cyclic sonata form, with common themes treated on the principle of variation'. Almost everything in the concerto is derived from the brief opening theme, or from the *cantabile* theme which opens the second section and gives birth to a number of highly contrasting variants, one of them forming the main theme of the final section.

Liszt dedicated his First Concerto to the Anglo-French Henry (or Henri) Litolff, the first composer regularly to treat the piano concerto as a symphony with piano *obbligato*. Of his five *Concertos symphoniques*, the first three directly influenced Liszt, and it may well be from Litolff that he got the idea of using the triangle in his First Concerto, a stroke which brought him much abuse. *The New Grove*, however, is mistaken

Hans von Bülow conducting a piano concerto, c. 1892.

in suggesting that Litolff was the first composer to use the triangle in a piano concerto. That honour went to the cloak-swirling Steibelt, who wrote a concerto for one piano, *two* orchestras and triangle in 1816. Litolff was, however, the first man to introduce the scherzo into the piano concerto, and it is for the scintillating Scherzo from his *Concerto symphonique* No. 4 alone that he is remembered today [CD 3].

Among the long-forgotten Romantic concertos which have recently been staging a comeback are examples by former household names such as Alkan, Bortkiewicz, d'Albert, Dussek, Field, Henselt, Herz, Lyapunov, Moscheles, Paderewski, Reinecke, Ries, Anton Rubinstein, Sauer and Scharwenka.

Of the serious Romantic concertos which have held their place in the repertoire, the best-known are by Schumann, Mendelssohn, Chopin, Weber (whose Konzertstück in F minor is written to a specific 'literary' programme), Liszt, Grieg, Tchaikovsky, Saint-Saëns and Rachmaninov, all of whom, with the sole exception of Liszt, fell back on the old Classical three-movement scheme, while retaining the standard Romantic concept of the soloist as hero. The piano concertos of Dvořák, Glazunov, Rimsky-Korsakov and Delius, despite the popularity of their composers in other respects, have never achieved more than curiosity status with the musical public at large.

The two piano concertos of Brahms are in a category of their own, both of them being of a size, length and seriousness unique at the time of their composition and unsurpassed since (except by Busoni's monstrosity of a concerto, complete with male chorus, which holds the record for sheer length and self-conscious grandiosity, clocking in at roughly an hour and twenty minutes). Both, too, hark back to Classical models, and both (particularly the Second) are of colossal difficulty. More than any other concertos of the Romantic era, these two great works engage the mind as much as the spirit. There is nothing, however, remotely arid or excessively cerebral in either. The canvas may be vast, but the paints are mixed by one of the greatest lyric song-writers in musical history. As a melodist, Brahms was at least the equal of his idol Beethoven, and his use of melodic ideas, his

Le Grand Concert. *Painting by Raoul Dufy, 1948.*

capacity to make them flower and develop, is hardly less wonderful. The Second, in B flat, is the only great concerto of the Romantic era to be cast in four movements, and is the most symphonic of all in scope and size. The 'extra' movement is a powerful scherzo, which Brahms unusually places second.

The most successful piano concertos of the twentieth century, apart from those of Rachmaninov, who continued to compose in a nineteenth-century idiom, are Bartók's three and Prokofiev's five (all of which emphasize the piano's percussive qualities and rely heavily for effect on their driving, exciting rhythms), two each from Ravel (one for the left hand alone) and Shostakovich (one for piano and trumpet), Falla's *Nights in the Gardens of Spain* and Gershwin's Concerto in F though this has never won the same popularity as the evergreen *Rhapsody in Blue.* The latter marked the first time that the idioms of so-called popular song were used as the definitive ingredients of a work for piano and orchestra, and in its episodic, haphazard nature – clear-cut sections can be dropped or rearranged with no significant loss to the effect of the whole – it may be seen as reflecting the disintegration of traditional values in the wake of the First World War. While much admired by many musicians, the concertos of Schoenberg,

Stravinsky, Britten, Tippett, Barber, Carter, Bennett and a goodly number of others have failed to find any lasting favour with audiences.

Of those concertos deliberately conceived in a 'modernist' idiom, the most consistently popular is probably the Prokofiev First [CD 3], whose stirring, attention-grabbing opening has the same kind of immediate appeal as Carl Orff's *Carmina Burana*. Like Liszt's concertos, its one-movement form is not a mere welding together of three discrete movements but a single, grandiose sonata design with some interesting and arresting deviations from tradition. In the words of the composer himself, it is 'a sonata *allegro* with the introduction repeated after the exposition and again at the end, and with a short *andante* before the development, the development taking the form of a scherzo and cadenza introducing the recapitulation'. If enjoyment of the work, however, depended on a recognition of these formal devices, the piece would never have gained even half its present popularity.

CHAPTER 10

Mechanomania

In anything at all, perfection is finally attained
not when there is no longer anything to add,
but when there is no longer anything to take away.

(Antoine de Saint-Exupéry)

To those who are never satisfied we owe our civilization. As the old Yiddish proverb has it, 'He who lies on the ground cannot fall.' That legion of craftsmen, designers, artists, tinkerers and crack-pots who have made the piano what it is today have never been guilty of lying on the ground. Nor even now have they given up their quest for the perfect instrument. In large part, they have made the piano what it is through their relentless attempts, over many generations, to make it what it is not. They have turned it into the biggest box of tricks in the history of music. On the face of it, nothing could be more unmusical, more unnatural, than an instrument whose every note

'The patent Dolce Campana pedal pianoforte', New York, c. 1850.

begins at its loudest and then rapidly fades away. Like the harpsichord which it largely replaced, it is an affront, in its very nature, to the concept of song. Yet makers and composers alike have unceasingly striven to make it sing. Unlike the harpsichord and organ, with their armoury of stops, the individual tones of the piano are, acoustically speaking, of a monotonous similarity, differing from one another in loudness, as the instrument's formal name suggests, but in little else. Yet composers, virtuosos and musical mechanics have tirelessly treated it as a surrogate orchestra. And it works. We buy the illusion.

We may. Certain of our ancestors did not. In their determined attempts to rid the instrument of its shortcomings, they turned, in effect, to genetic engineering. Nor are the reasons hard to divine. Throughout the eighteenth and nineteenth centuries, the great majority of music lovers lacked either the opportunity or the wherewithal to attend orchestral concerts, let alone the opera. For many, the closest they were ever likely to get was through the domestic performance of symphonic and operatic reductions. It was to this end, among others, that Liszt made his quite extraordinary transcriptions of major orchestral works such as the Beethoven symphonies and Berlioz's *Symphonie Fantastique*. And he was by no means alone, save for the brilliance of his musical syntheses.

For home consumption, not only single works but whole concert programmes were issued in keyboard transcriptions, with indications of their original instrumental dress, so that the pianist could try and 'imitate' the sound of flutes, cellos or massed brass as circumstances required. Since the piano is manifestly unsuited to such evocations, and in response to the public mania for two- and four-hand reductions of orchestral and operatic works, domestic instruments were frequently encumbered by a battery of special effects.

Many of these excrescences derived from the extraordinary vogue for 'Turkish' military music which convulsed much of Europe in the eighteenth and early nineteenth centuries, and of which Mozart's famous *Rondo alla turca* (from his Piano Sonata in A, K331), the finale of his Fifth Violin Concerto, and his opera *The Seraglio* are the noblest symptoms. But there were other, more immediate sources. Given humanity's deep-rooted enthusiasm for programmatic music (evident even in the rituals of the Stone Age, with their imitations of animals and birds), it should come as no surprise that the revolutionary period from 1776 to 1815 saw a dramatic increase in the number of militaristic pieces, the most famous being Beethoven's *Wellington's Victory, or the Battle of Vittoria* (one of the most meretricious pot-boilers ever to come from the pen of a great composer), which he himself arranged for piano. Another, already noted, was František Kotzwara's runaway best-seller *The Battle of Prague*, whose artillery was still resounding in the early years of the twentieth century.

Internal view of an upright piano by Ehrlich, c. 1820.

But while Beethoven and the hapless Kotzwara may have commanded the heights, they were only two of a multitude that included Steibelt, whose stock-in-trade was his eerie *tremolando* (and who has been credited with establishing the tambourine and drum pedals as a popular addition to the piano), the aforementioned Wanhal (*The Battle of Würzburg*) and even Hummel, whose curiously styled *Battle-Coda for the Apollo Rooms* sits uneasily with his outspoken attacks on the use of supernumerary pedals for purposes of programmatic sound effects. The apotheosis of this development came with a curious attempt in the mid-nineteenth century to incorporate into the main body of the piano a panoply of tambourines and kettledrums tuned to the chromatic scale, and the extraordinary 'piano basque' of Paul-Joseph

Sormani in Paris, which consisted entirely of tambourines whose 'beaters' were operated by a keyboard. Nor was this craze confined to the vulgar lower orders. From William Gardiner we learn that the Earl of Sandwich (he of the eponymous luncheon) 'was so enamoured with the thunder of the drums [captured at the Battle of Dettingen in 1743] that he had one side of his music-room strained with parchment, which being suddenly struck upon, so alarmed the company as to throw many into fits, which his Lordship maintained was certain proof of the boldness of the effect'. How he would have applauded the piano with chromatic kettledrums devised in 1847 by Messrs Nunn and Fischer of New York 'so that strings and drums could be sounded simultaneously' (though how they managed to accommodate the sheer bulk of the drums required for the bass register is difficult to imagine). Also of interest was a piano built by John Jacob Astor (an instrument maker and dealer before bagging his first million in the fur trade), boasting a special pedal which lifted the instrument's lid, originally for purposes of swelling the sound. If the pedal were released suddenly, however, the lid would descend with a satisfying crash (an item of pianistic armoury denied to your average piano-stool strategist).

It would be wrong to suppose that the ingenuity of the inventor's imagination was confined to this sort of ephemera. There were serious drawbacks intrinsic to the piano's design which exercised the minds even of the greatest and most esteemed makers. One, later overcome, was the lack of power common to all the earliest models. Another, still awaiting solution, was the instrument's inability to sustain the strength or to control the tone of a note once the hammer had hit the strings. It was in the hope of solving this defect in particular that many of the most ingenious modifications of the piano were designed. Some of the earliest were aimed directly at the (theoretically) straightforward combination of the piano with its most relentlessly tone-sustaining relative, the organ. No less a maker than Johann Stein of Augsburg (lavishly praised, as we have seen, by the normally ungenerous Mozart), turned out a number of experimental hybrids. En route to his 'Melodika', or 'clavecin organisée' of 1783 – a combination piano and touch-sensitive reed organ – he had devised, in 1769, a combined harpsichord and fortepiano to which he gave the modest name of 'Polytoni-clavichordium', and another cross-breed, the charmingly named 'Vis-à-vis Flügel': a one-manual piano combined with a three-manual harpsichord, and requiring two players to operate it.

Such modest experiments as these, however, were soon eclipsed by more ambitious conceits. Thirteen years after Stein unveiled his 'Melodika', the little-known Still Brothers made a once-in-a-lifetime bid for immortality with a combined piano and organ housing 230 strings, 360 pipes and 105 different tonal accoutrements, including bells, drums, cymbals, triangles and fully 25 pedals, designed to unleash a further armoury of special effects, including lute, flute, bassoon, viola da gamba, French horn and clarinet. Not to be outdone, one Zink of Hesse-Homburg commissioned in 1800 a three-manual extravaganza comprising no fewer than 14 instruments, among them, in addition to grand piano and organ, a glass harmonica and a full-size wind band. And for those intimidated by so excessive a brandishing of soulless technology, Johann Völler of Angersbach sugared the pill by including in his own piano-cum-organ a delicately fashioned automaton in the shape of a flute-playing eight-year-old boy, who decorously removed the instrument from his lips during the rests. All this, however, pales into insignificance next to the instrument's most revolutionary innovation: a device administering electric shocks to the performer, though to what end we are left to surmise.

In the battle to secure a sustained tone for the piano (and before it, the harpsichord), perhaps the most curious experiments have been those aimed at actually bowing the strings. The earliest known device of this kind dates from as early as 1570. In 1742 a French maker incorporated into a harpsichord a cello and viola, the bowing of which was controlled by treadles, the 'bows' themselves consisting of rollers wrapped in horse-hair. Seven years later, he extended the principle and expanded the orchestra to include two violins and a drum. Another instrument, from 1764, included a built-in lute and consort of viols.

Of all tone-sustaining experiments, none exceeded in originality

M. Schalkenbach demonstrates his electric 'Piano-Orchestra' in 1862.

or impracticality the so-called 'Animo-Corde' which sought, on the model of the Aeolian harp, to prolong the strings' vibrations by carefully channelled currents of air. The 'Animo-Corde', however, was not an isolated phenomenon. In 1842 in Paris, Matthieu-François Isoard devised a scheme in which a movable box, containing as many compartments as there were strings to be vibrated, was positioned beneath the strings, each compartment being connected by means of a valve to a wind box. A separate container took in compressed air from a double bellows, operated by keys which likewise controlled the passage of air out of the bellows and over the strings. More curious yet was an instrument invented by Henri Pape of Paris which dispensed with the strings altogether, substituting in their place various springs, of steel, copper, brass and any number of other metals, depending on the quality of tone desired. For as long as the sustained tone of a given note was required, the springs would be kept in a state of almost uniform vibration by means of a toothed barrel with a speed of repetition far beyond the capacity of the human hand. The result was apparently more like a vocal or violinistic vibrato than the guitar-like repeated notes found in Scarlatti and Ravel.

A parallel line of development, almost literally, was the quest for a soundboard which would maximize the resonance of the vibrating strings. In 1812, Erard, in Paris, brought out a giraffe-like upright

fitted with a cylindrical soundboard to which a second keyboard
could be fitted or removed at will.
Thirteen years later, another
Frenchman, Étienne Eulriot,
patented an ellipse-shaped piano
with two circular soundboards,
one at either end.

A quite different line of pursuit had been initiated in 1797 by
a pair of English makers, Messrs
Rolfe and Davis, who dispensed
with the wooden soundboard

*Friedrich Kaufmann and family demonstrate their
pianos to Queen Victoria in 1851.*

altogether, replacing it with a resonating surface of parchment. The
experiment was not a success, but the model of the drum was not
forgotten. In the middle 1830s, a number of makers, inspired by the
sonorous depth of the timpani, adapted not only the resonating head
of the drum but the bowl itself. The idea was first floated in 1834 by
Georges Frédéric Greiner, whose suprapianistic obsessions also
resulted in the bizarre 'Pianoforte on the Principle of the Speaking
Trumpet', and later in the same year, that tireless tinkerer Henri Pape
patented a circular piano with a soundboard in the form of a kettle-
drum, copper bowl and all.

Not that France was the only theatre of operations on this front.
In a positive fever of complexity, one D. C. Hewitt of London,
attempting in 1844 to equalize the tension on the frame, patented a
piano with strings on both sides of the soundboard. In order to
produce the optimum sound, each key acted upon not one hammer
but six (three on each side), so co-ordinated that they all struck their
strings at precisely the same moment.

And of course there were peripheral developments, some directly
reflecting the preponderantly amateur status of those who bought and
played the instruments. Among the most elaborate of these concessions
to the market place were various makes of 'transposing pianos', a

development warmly welcomed by the editor of *The Musical Herald* in 1846:

> A performer, who, on the ordinary pianoforte, can play only on the easiest keys, may, by means of this invention, produce the same sounds as if he was playing on the most difficult keys. For example, the Funeral March in Beethoven's Op. 26 is in the key of *A flat minor*, with *seven* flats. By lowering the pitch of the instrument by a semitone, and playing *from the same notes*, the *very same sounds* will be produced from the white keys which were previously produced from the black. It would, indeed, be necessary, on the occasional occurrence of an *accidental natural*, to change it mentally to a *sharp*, but the small difficulty thence arising would only be an improving exercise to the learner.

A further wrinkle was devised by Mr D. C. Hewitt, he of the six-hammer key stroke, who was the first to invent an additional keyboard to be placed over the ordinary one for transposing.

A number of composers welcomed the arrival of the transposing piano, if only as an antidote to the publishers' then common practice of printing works in unauthorized transpositions to 'easier' keys, for the benefit of parlour operatives unable to effect the changes for themselves. Schubert's beautiful G flat Impromptu (six flats) was widely published throughout the nineteenth century in the key of G major (one sharp), the irony being that while it may be easier to read in that key, it is substantially more difficult to play.

From time to time, attempts have been made to adapt the keyboard itself to the natural, lateral movement of the arms, that is to say in a curved line rather than a straight one. Despite the successive failures scored by all such aberrations, the idea has been floated in one generation after another, ever since the Viennese piano maker Neuhaus first wheeled it out in 1780. Two other Austrians, Staufer and Haidinger, took out a patent on their own variant in 1824, to be followed by other inventive hopefuls in 1840, and again in the late 1860s. It wasn't until the second decade of the twentieth century, however, that the day of the concave keyboard looked like dawning at last. In 1910, a German named Clutsam succeeded in persuading a number of leading manufacturers to adapt and market his own version, which enjoyed a flurry of celebrity when certain reputable artists played on it in public, leading to its eventual, if brief, adoption by the *Königliche Hochschule für Musik* in Berlin. As its only real beneficiaries were children and diminutive women (who could now reach octaves and tenths with ease), it soon fell out of favour and joined its predecessors on the scrap heap.

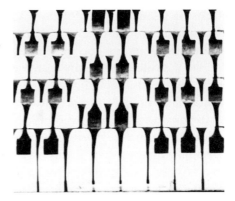

Detail of the Janko keyboard of an upright piano by Decker, New York, c. 1890.

More fruitful, and marginally longer-lived, have been the various attempts at extending the piano's range and versatility by means of pedal keyboards, on the model of the organ. The Metropolitan Museum in New York houses one such instrument, built by Johann Stein of Augsburg as early as 1778, and in the first half of the nineteenth century both Erard and Pleyel experimented with the idea in Paris. On both sides of the Atlantic, the pedal keyboard attracted some distinguished advocates. In 1843, Louis Schöne constructed a pedal piano for Felix Mendelssohn, comprising 29 notes and connected to a separate action, placed at the back of an upright, where a special soundboard covered with 29 strings was built into the case. Whatever its virtues, however, this promising hybrid was never a really viable proposition, and would probably have sunk without trace had Robert Schumann not written some of his loveliest pieces for it. No serious lover of piano music should be ignorant of his beautiful *Études in the Form of Canons*, or of Debussy's equally beautiful arrangement of them for two pianos. Their neglect by duo-piano teams is hard to understand.

Far and away the most imaginative and truly musical experiment with the keyboard was conducted by a fiercely moustachioed Hungarian nobleman in the 1880s. Paul von Janko was himself an accomplished pianist, a graduate both of the Vienna Conservatory and the Polytechnicum, and the possessor of a restless and enquiring mind. Far from being a dotty gadgeteer, he was the first man thoroughly to re-examine the very principles of the conventional keyboard, whose layout had been essentially unchanged for more than 400 years – four centuries of cataclysmic change in the evolution of European music. Moved by a desire to bring the most difficult modern works within the grasp of the serious amateur, he devised a multiple keyboard of several tiers, similar in appearance to that of the organ, but closer in principle to the then new-fangled typewriter (invented in Milwaukee, Wisconsin in 1867). With this ingenious device, adaptable to any piano with a normal action, such wide-spanned intervals as the tenth and even the twelfth could be played with ease, simply by moving a finger to the rank immediately above or below the principal keyboard in use at the time. Making child's play of virtuoso barnstormers, however, was a dangerous business. If Granny or little Emma could dash off Liszt's *La Campanella* in the family parlour after tea, what price the heroic accomplishments of a Rubinstein, Tausig or Bülow? The publishers, fearing that widespread adoption of the Janko keyboard would depreciate their stock, since naturally everything would have to be refingered, implacably opposed the invention. Hordes of imperilled teachers equally deplored it. Piano manufacturers, too, were thrown into a quandary. The chips were down. Despite sympathetic advocacy by no less a manufacturer than Blüthner, Janko didn't stand a chance. By the outbreak of World War I in 1914, his brainchild was all but officially declared dead. By the time the German Paul Perzina devised his brilliant 'Reversible Key-Bottom' (by means of which the Janko as well as the conventional keyboard could be used on the same piano), it was too late. Janko adjourned to Constantinople, where he died a disappointed man in 1919. But as one commentator put it at the time, he had got his bearings wrong. The commonest failings of pianistic lions were not technical but musical. What was called for was 'a patent mind attachment for brainless virtuosi'. For the curious, a working example of Janko's invention may be seen at the National Museum in Washington D.C.

Like Janko, Emanuel Moór was both Hungarian and an accomplished, even distinguished musician – a pianist and a prolific composer who had works commissioned by the likes of Ysaÿe, Casals and Flesch. His 'Duplex Coupler Grand Piano', unveiled in 1921, was effectively two pianos in a single case, tuned an octave apart, with two manuals, as on the harpsichord, which could be played separately or in combination, thus enabling the pianist to play such masterworks as Bach's Goldberg Variations (written for double-manual harpsichord) without recourse to tricks and compromise. The inventor's British wife, Winifred Christie, made an excellent recording of Bach's famous Toccata and Fugue in D minor on the Moór Piano, as it was more simply known, but despite such convincing evidence of its merits and the warm recommendation of Sir Donald Tovey, the instrument was too limited in scope, too ungainly to behold and too difficult to play. It was quickly forgotten, but a surviving example can still be seen, by special arrangement, at the Royal Academy of Music in London. These so-called 'duoclave' instruments made sporadic appearances throughout the second quarter of the nineteenth century, and were sometimes no more than two pianos, be they square or 'grand', housed in a single rectangular frame.

Wherever the piano has flourished, a cluster of curious mutations has inevitably arisen, including such improbable items as the 'Portable Grand Pianos' marketed by London's Longman & Broderip in 1789, or their smaller cousins which could 'be conveyed and even played on in a coach'. Mozart's friend Michael Kelly recalled that the Duke of Queensberry owned one of the latter and was seldom seen to travel without it. From other sources we learn of carriages with mini-pianos fitted under the seats, to be withdrawn and played at opportune moments, just as we hear of other diminutive pianos accompanying singers on the waterways of Venice. In 1836, a Parisian maker patented a piano so small and ingeniously hinged that it could be folded away in a case and taken on journeys along with conventional baggage. With the keyboard folded away, the thickness was a mere seven inches. Three years later, also in Paris, Henri Pape knocked a further six inches off the height, reducing it to 2 feet 9 inches. The most revolutionary of all nineteenth-century developments, however, was concerned neither with size nor with such fundamental pianistic accoutrements as keyboards and resonators. It threatened to make pianists themselves redundant.

*   *   *

To have music without effort is one of humanity's oldest dreams. Attempts to realize it go back a long way, probably into prehistory. In ancient China and India there were several kinds of Aeolian harps, whose strings were sounded by the wind. In Malaysia the wind was used to produce sound from bamboo pipes, and in the paddy-fields of Indonesia, water in the irrigation channels knocks tuned bamboo tubes against stones, thereby producing a continuous kaleidoscope of melody and rhythms. The music created by these ancient devices was necessarily of a very random nature. The first attempt to control automatic instruments seems to have been made by three brothers in Baghdad in the ninth century AD, and the principle they explored became the basis of virtually all mechanical music making for the next thousand years. The same idea was further elaborated by Leonardo da Vinci in the fifteenth century, and by the time of Henry VIII, who had a self-playing virginal, it had reached a considerable degree of sophistication. It involved a rotating cylinder, studded with little pins which, in the case of the virginal, raised and dropped the keys of a keyboard.

It was with the advent of watch making in the early sixteenth century that mechanical music making really took off. Within the lifetime of Elizabeth I, Henry's automatic virginal was already an antique. In 1599, the queen sent to the Sultan of Turkey an extravagantly complicated mechanical organ and carillon, operated by a clock with a 24-hour striking mechanism. As time passed, musical clocks grew steadily more sophisticated. No less a composer than Haydn composed pieces for them, and it was for a mechanical barrel organ that Mozart composed one of his keyboard masterpieces, the great Fantasia in F minor, K608 – often, and understandably, commandeered by pianists.

In 1805, the much respected musician and historian Dr Charles Burney reported that 'recent improvements have rendered the barrel capable of producing an effect equal to the fingers of the first-rate performers'. Good news for the barrel merchants, unsettling news for performers. And the barrel had plans for the composer too. Ever since the mid-seventeenth century there had been sporadic attempts to take the effort out of the composing as well as the playing of music. The famous diarist Pepys had a composing machine which can still be seen at the Pepysian Museum in Cambridge. And there were similar devices on the continent. For those who were not mechanically minded, one London publisher, late in the eighteenth century, produced an interesting alternative, namely 'A Tabular System whereby Any Person, without the Least Knowledge of Music, may compose Ten Thousand Minuets in the most pleasing and correct manner'. The prospective buyer may well have decided that it was better after all to stick to machines.

In 1821, a Dutchman, one Dietrich Nikolaus Winkel, produced what he called a 'Componium'. Three years later a celebrated musical theorist and a respected scientist investigated this contraption and jointly issued a report:

> When this instrument has received a varied theme, which the inventor has had time to fix by a process involving pins and barrels, it decomposes the variations of itself, and reproduces their parts in all the orders of possible permutation ... None of the airs which it varies lasts above a minute; could it be supposed that but one of these was played without interruption, yet through the principle of variability which it possesses, it might, without ever resuming precisely the same combination, continue to play not only during years and ages but during so immense a *series* of ages that, though the figures might be brought to express them, common language could not.

Contemporaneous with the 'Componium' was the tongue-twisting 'Kaleidacousticon', by means of which, to quote an advertisement, 'upwards of 214,000,000 waltzes may be composed'. So much for a mere 10,000 minuets. Since the marketers of these machines seem to have been obsessed with numbers, it might be worth noting that at the rate of ten waltzes a day it would take just upwards of 58,630 years to dance through the lot, leaving you little time in which to savour the fruits of a different technology that was to change the face of domestic music making for ever.

Among the more eccentric and visionary pioneers of music on tap was a certain G. P. Hackenburg, who in 1865 came up with a refreshingly original if somewhat impractical idea:

> I have determined, by means of electricity, to supply every house with music, just as it is with gas and water, by means of pipes. About the middle of the town I propose to erect a central station – the music manufactory. It will include a piano as the machine, and a first-rate pianist to play it. Everyone who subscribes will be provided with a piano. Every such piano will be connected by electric wires to the central piano, so that when my distinguished pianist plays the overture to *Don Giovanni*, with the utmost virtuosity and the deepest feeling, all the pianos connected with the central one will perform the overture at the same time and in the same manner. If the demand is great, I shall have the playing go on day and night. It is only necessary to put on a metal stopper and the melodies will continue to flow in uninterrupted joyousness.

As it happens, Hackenburg's strange dream came very close to being realized, but by a quite different method, and not by himself. In 1825, in London, the esteemed firm of Clementi, Collard & Collard produced a machine that marked a new chapter in the story of the piano, though its full import was not perceived at the time. One critic wrote:

> This curious instrument, furnished with a horizontal cylinder similar to that of a barrel organ, and put into motion by a steel spring, performs without external force or manual operation, the most difficult and intricate compositions. When the spring is fully wound up, it will act for more than half an hour, and may be again prepared for performance in half a minute, and if required, stopped in an instant while in full action.

Speed may be regulated at pleasure, while *piano, forte, sforzato* and *diminuendo* are produced by the slightest motion of the hand applied to a sliding ball at the side of the instrument.

As so often happens with inventions, the same sort of thing had been dreamt up simultaneously by a man named Courcell, and was manufactured in the same year under the fashionably Greek-sounding name of 'Cylindrichord'. It was operated by a crank at the side, and won fulsome praise from a respected English musician, Dr Thomas Busby, who rather blew his cover by declaring 'The Cylindrichord is an admirable and efficient substitute for a first-rate performer on the pianoforte.' Both these inventions sound uncannily like the player-pianos which seriously threatened to put the conventional piano out of business at the start of the twentieth century, except that the Cylindrichord operated by means of clockwork and they worked on the principle of the automatic loom. The latter involved a perforated card on a cylinder, which allowed certain needles to pass through it while rejecting others. It was only a matter of time before someone realized that the same principle could be applied to air pumped by a bellows. By this means, musical instruments too could be controlled.

In the case of the piano or the organ, the pressure of the air would determine the movement of the keys.

Advertisement for a pianola, 1914.

It wasn't until 1863 that the first complete pneumatic player-piano was built and patented, and even then it was a dramatic failure. By the late 1870s the idea had begun to intrigue tinkerers on both sides of the Atlantic, but the public steadfastly refused to take it seriously. Ten years later there were a number of machines on the market whose sophistication left the Cylindrichord way behind, yet still the public proved unready. By the turn of the century, however, both machinery and public had begun significantly to change. In the case of the machines, the crank was replaced by a twin-pedalled footpump, leaving the operator's hands free to manipulate other controls, which affected speed and volume. The feet too were brought into play, one operating the pump which controlled the bellows, the other controlling the sustaining pedal. Theoretically, the consumer could now be offered a virtuoso technique, unlimited repertoire and a high degree of interpretative control – and at no expense of effort. The manufacturers were on to a good thing, and they knew it. The standard sales pitch was typified by an advertisement which appeared in an Ohio newspaper in 1905:

> PERFECTION WITHOUT PRACTICE!
> Yours at last! How many thousands of American parlors contain that shining monument to a past girlhood – a silent piano? Do you wish to *enjoy* your piano? This can now be accomplished, by owning a Cecilian Piano Player!

But could it? The fact is that the player-piano only made bad piano playing easier. To most musically sensitive ears, it continued to sound as mechanical as it unarguably was. Hackenburg's vision of getting first-class piano playing into every home remained a pipe-dream. But not for long.

Having dealt, as they believed, with the matter of technique, the manufacturers now turned their attention to removing the effort from interpretation as well. Rolls soon appeared with specific but anonymous guidelines dictating precisely how the tempo and rhythm of any given piece should be controlled. By 1905 these rudimentary instructions were increasingly replaced by ready-made interpretations, authorized by world-famous pianists. Follow their suggestions, went the message, and you could have Paderewski in your parlour. So said the theory. The reality said otherwise, as most connoisseurs agreed. But then came the breakthrough.

A German called Welte invented a device by means of which a piano roll, properly perforated, could record with a high degree of fidelity performances given by living pianists. Hackenburg's dream was soon to be realized. Welte called his invention the 'Mignon' and soon persuaded many of the greatest pianists and composers of the day to record on it. It was a turning point in musical history. In 1905, 6 per cent of the pianos sold in the United States were player-pianos. Within a decade the percentage had more than quadrupled, and a mere five years after that the figure had risen to 70 per cent. Accordingly, fewer and fewer people learned to play the conventional piano. There was no doubt about it: the centuries-old tradition of genuinely home-made music was in big trouble. But it couldn't all be blamed on the player-piano. The most significant changes affecting the state of music were not, in fact, technological but social.

A Duo-Art Pianola playing with the Queen's Hall Orchestra under Sir Henry Wood in 1922.

Coda

As the nineteenth century turned uneventfully into the twentieth, increasing numbers of women, particularly educated, middle-class women, were growing restive. For a century and a half, as we have seen, women in the middle class had been bred as genteel adornments of a predominantly masculine, market-based society. The militant activities of the suffragettes in the early years of the new century stimulated many women to question the values that had effectively clipped their wings for as long as anyone could remember. Those values, however, were about to be badly shaken by a cataclysm more terrible than anything the suffragettes could have devised. In 1914, with the outbreak of the First World War, society was to be changed for ever – and one of the most radical changes was in the

*Recording a punched paper roll
for use on a pianola, 1909.*

status of women. When the war finished in 1918, women on both sides
of the Atlantic, in belated recognition of their wartime services, were
granted the right to vote – and with it they were at least partially
freed from the tyranny of past expectations. They could now go out
to work and go to university; they could finally wear comfortable
clothes, they could travel freely, and stood at least a chance of
remaining single without shame.

The purely social aspect of music in the home was devalued,
virtually overnight. The player-piano succeeded quite as dramatically
as it did largely because it filled a sudden gap. Freed at last from
the shackles of 'accomplishments', Greta, Françoise and Jane had
pianistically decamped. But there were other forces at work. High
among the long-term casualties of the war was the role of the home
as a social centre. During the so-called Roaring Twenties, restaurants
and nightclubs proliferated at a fantastic rate. Servants were increasingly difficult to find, and in any case a home-centred life was
beginning to become a symbol of a largely discredited past. But the
home was destabilized by technology too. The cinema drew people
out in droves, and improvements in contraception brought about
major changes in the nature of the family unit itself. The sprawling
broods of Victorian times were relegated, by and large, to the yellowing
pages of the photograph album. In all this great sea of change, music
lost much of its traditional, practical value. It ceased to be regarded

Recording the piano in the 1890s.

as a stepping-stone to the altar, and there was no longer much call for it as a social adhesive. Indeed it looked in serious danger of reverting after several centuries to the status of a mere art, to be appreciated and cultivated, if it was cultivated at all, for its own sake. But increasing numbers of the sincerest music lovers saw no reason to cultivate it – not, at least, to the extent of actually learning how to write for or play it. That need had been largely eroded, first by the player-piano – and then by a still more remarkable invention whose progress had been almost as slow.

As long ago as 1877, almost half a century before the height of the player-piano boom, a young ex-newsboy named Thomas Edison was tinkering with an improvement of the telegraph, when he discovered, without having ever set out to, that it might be possible to preserve and reproduce the sound of the human voice. He called his invention the phonograph, and with its subsequent development the first nail looked to have been hammered into the coffin of the piano.

But had it? The fact is that piano recitals, piano concertos and virtuoso displays of almost every kind have continued to fascinate the musical public throughout the social and technological upheavals of the twentieth century. Pianists continue to abound. Indeed there are probably more first-rate pianists in the world today than at any other time since the instrument's invention – most of them ignored by the big record companies and the high-profile promoters who have largely replaced the enlightened and chance-taking impresarios of former times (though these, it must be admitted, were never very numerous). The piano itself has remained much as it was in the great days of Rubinstein and Paderewski, and claims that the most advanced electronic instruments now rival the concert grand in quality and range have failed to gain credence not only with practising musicians but with the musical public at large. The same can be said of the modifications effected by a small but well-publicized minority of mid-twentieth-century composers such as the Americans Henry Cowell, Lou Harrison, Christian Wolff and John Cage, and the much admired Japanese composer Toshiro Mayuzumi. Each of these has experimented with the use of the so-called 'prepared piano', placing various foreign objects (rubber erasers, mutes, nuts, bolts, screws, spoons, hatpins and so on) between or on top of the strings, in some cases with quite captivating results – Cage's *Sonatas and Interludes* being perhaps the best-known case in point. Less seductive is his *Water Music* of 1952, in which the pianist is required to pour water from pots, blow whistles under water, use a radio and a pack of cards, and other similar diversions. Novel sonorities have also been produced by sticking drawing pins in the hammers (no less an artist than the late Glenn Gould experimented with this, dubbing his own particular mutation the *harpsipiano*).

To many, such assaults on the instrument's painstakingly achieved physiology have seemed an intolerable indignity. Nor could the great makers, from Broadwood to Bösendorfer, have anticipated a time when the modern grand would be banished from the concert platform in favour of the very instrument whose limitations they had devoted their lives to overcoming. Yet this has been the inevitable result of the mania for musicological authenticity which has gripped large sections of the musical world in the final decades of the twentieth century. Interestingly, none of the world's greatest pianists has yet seen fit to embrace the fortepiano as his or her instrument of choice when it comes to the playing of Mozart, Haydn, Beethoven or Schubert, and it would appear that the majority of music lovers share this scepticism. Only when the likes of Alfred Brendel, Murray Perahia, Radu Lupu, Daniel Barenboim, Richard Goode and Maurizio Pollini take up the older instrument will the authenticists have won the day.

And what of the repertoire? Despite the impressive and impassioned advocacy of such pianists as Pollini, Michel Béroff, Paul Crossley and Peter Serkin, most of the piano music written since the serialist revolution initiated by Schoenberg in the early years of the twentieth century has found little or no favour with that great majority of piano players who are not professionals. This is only partly due to the great technical difficulty which characterizes much of it. No such reason can explain the persistent unpopularity of works like Schoenberg's *Six Little Pieces*, Op. 19, pianistically among the most uncomplicated pieces ever written by a great composer.

But the story of the piano is far from over. Its halcyon days are gone, perhaps, yet at the time of writing, the piano market is holding steady, and pianists maintain their central place both in the concert hall and the recording studio. Thousands of pianists graduate each year from music colleges and conservatories in the United States alone. Few of them will achieve fame and fortune as performers, yet few of them will lack pupils. And the very rise of technology which looked at one point like putting the piano out of business may well contribute to its revival in the home. As the Age of Leisure takes hold, as more and more people have less and less to do and are increasingly forced by circumstance to re-evaluate themselves and their lives, the piano may yet regain a significant role in the everyday experience of ordinary people. Reports of its death, as of Mark Twain's, have been greatly exaggerated.

APPENDIX

Gradus ad Parnassum

Supplementary observations relating to some of the artists
represented on CDs 1–3

Please note: On the CDs which accompany this volume a number of
recordings made in the earlier years of the gramophone have been
included. In one or two cases, the standard of reproduction is noticeably
inferior to that which would normally be expected today, and there is a
certain amount of background 'hiss' deriving from the original 78 r.p.m
discs. This is particularly noticeable in the tracks devoted to Alfred
Cortot (recorded under wartime conditions in 1943), Vladimir Horowitz
(in 1934 still not 30 years old), and Artur Rubinstein (playing in 1928,
only two years after the introduction of electrical recording), but we
feel that it is a small price to pay for the unique quality of these
historic performances.

Edwin Fischer (1886–1960), J. S. Bach and the Piano – CD 1.
There is something pleasingly appropriate in the title of J. S. Bach's
Das Wohltemperierte Clavier (The Well-tempered Clavier). 'Clavier',
unlike the more precise labels of clavichord, harpsichord or organ, is
a generic term, embracing all keyboard instruments. This astonishing
collection of 48 Preludes and Fugues, one of the greatest monuments
of human endeavour, was not specifically composed for the piano, but
along with Bach's other keyboard works it stands as the bedrock on
which the whole history of piano music is based (the suites of his exact
contemporary Handel have never found a central place in pianists'
affections, and the harpsichord sonatas of Scarlatti are a unique
flowering of genius without any offspring of immediate consequence).

Consisting of two books, each containing a Prelude and Fugue in
every key (in chromatically ascending order: C major–C minor, C
sharp major–C sharp minor etc.), *The Well-tempered Clavier*, also known

as 'The 48', is both a compendium of Bach's unparalleled keyboard art and a celebration of the then still recent system of 'equal temperament', in which the octave is divided into twelve equal semitones, thus allowing transposition into any key without recourse to retuning (a necessity with all instruments tuned according to the once universal practice of 'natural temperament'. Fortunately, the work is entirely free of the prolixity accruing to its full title, which may be translated into English as

> *The Well-tempered Clavier*, or Preludes and Fugues through all tones and semitones, relating to the major third, that is Ut Re Mi, as well as those relating to the minor third, that is Re Mi Fa, compiled and prepared for the benefit and practice of young musicians desirous of learning, as well as for the entertainment of those already versed in this particular study, by Johann Sebastian Bach, Anno 1722.

Until the advent of recording, Bach's keyboard works were known more or less exclusively to those who could play them. It was only with Edwin Fischer's historic recording of the complete *Well-tempered Clavier* in the 1930s that this state of affairs was laid to rest. When Fischer was born, in Switzerland in 1886, Bach as a keyboard composer was best known, if known at all, by a handful of extravagantly romanticized arrangements which turned up in the recitals of bravura virtuosos. It was Fischer more than any other great pianist who repeatedly demonstrated to a wide musical public that it was possible, on the piano, to breathe life into all of Bach's keyboard music without recourse to the arranger's paintbrush. When he died in 1960 he had introduced two generations and more to a Bach who spoke not as a monument, nor as some respect-worthy museum piece, but as a living human being.

He did it, in part, by combining a highly cultivated musicianship and a profound understanding of his instrument with a passionate awareness that respect is worth nothing in art if it isn't born of love. As both man and musician, Fischer exuded a self-forgetfulness whose radiant humility was an inspiration to all who experienced it. In the words of one pupil, 'he made us better than we were'. His unbounded reverence for Bach never found more eloquent expression on disc than in the B minor Prelude and Fugue that concludes Book I of the *Well-tempered Clavier,* where one comes face to face with the composer himself, in all his simplicity, complexity and eternal nobility. And who, having heard it, can seriously dispute the suitability of the piano as a vehicle for Bachian counterpoint?

Artur Schnabel (1882–1951) – CD 1. Schnabel's became a name which in some circles you uttered in hushed tones of reverence or not at all. Such, indeed, was the devotion of some worshippers, born too late to have heard him in person, that they actually incorporated the great man's wrong notes, as culled from gramophone records, into their own performances.

Schnabel decided early in life to devote himself exclusively to those works which, in his own words, were 'better than they can be played'. His reputation as a pianist rests basically on five composers – Mozart, Beethoven, Schubert, Schumann and Brahms – and on the freshness and depth of his musical insights. In his pursuit of musical truth he became increasingly unconcerned with keyboard accuracy. No one was less bothered by this than Schnabel himself (whose favourite motto was 'Safety last!'). Once, during the recording of a Beethoven concerto, he played with exceptional conviction and illumination but dropped notes by the bushel. The conductor, noting this, suggested that it might be better if they tried again. 'It might be better,' said Schnabel. 'But it wouldn't be as good.'

Despite his dislike of recording, he became in the 1930s the first pianist to commit all of the 32 Beethoven sonatas to disc. His recordings of Mozart were rarer, but his playing of the A minor Rondo has become a classic in the history of the gramophone.

Solomon (1902–88) – CD 1. At the age of 12 Solomon was already a veteran of the concert platform who had spent a third of his young life as an established fixture on the English musical scene. His surname was Cutner but from the outset of his career he was known to the public by his first name alone.

From the beginning, one of the most remarkable features of Solomon's playing was its economy. As a measure of his faith in the power of music to express itself he would hold with an almost metronomic accuracy to his chosen tempi, and he avoided, on the whole, all extremes of contrast. Yet within these apparently strict confines he found an infinite variety of nuance which saved him from ever sounding remotely mechanical. In one sense he was a true Classicist who found in clarity of form an innately expressive meaning, but he was also, in the best Romantic tradition of the nineteenth century, a true pianist who loved his instrument not simply as a servant of music but unashamedly for its own sake. He valued and perfected the art of piano playing to a degree reached by few but his virtuosity was undemonstrative to a point which struck many as self-effacing, if not downright austere.

Solomon rarely fell short of the highest standards in any music, and his recordings of Chopin, Liszt, Schubert, Brahms and Debussy command the respect, and repay the attention, of serious music students everywhere. It is as a player of Mozart and Beethoven, how-ever, that he remains, in the view of very many people, quite simply unequalled, despite the fact that more than 40 years have elapsed since his final performance.

In 1956, and by general consent at the height of his powers, Solomon suffered a massive stroke that left his right side permanently paralysed and his speech seriously impaired. He lived on for another three decades, suffering a series of further strokes, discomforts and privations, and though he ended his years unable either to move or to speak, he had never been known to utter a single complaint from the time of his first stroke to the time of his death.

Few epitaphs could be more moving than his recording of Beethoven's last sonata, in which suffering and struggle are ultimately resolved in that 'peace that passeth all understanding' which Beethoven conveyed perhaps more perfectly than any other composer in the history of the piano.

Alfred Cortot (1877–1962) – CD 2. Born in Switzerland, Cortot was never just a pianist. In a lifetime of extraordinary industry, he wrote several books, founded and directed for several decades a celebrated school, edited volumes of music still in widespread use, and served in a department of the French government. His repertoire was vast, but in the public imagination he was associated above all with two composers, closely related in outlook and occasionally even in style. One was Chopin, the other Debussy, and his playing of both had much in common. What singled him out from most of the Romantics of his generation was neither his capacity for feeling nor the particular intensity of his vision, both of which were remarkable, but rather the intellectual discipline with which he clarified the emotional essence of a work (a discipline not always extended to his fingers: especially in later years, he was almost as well known for his technical mishaps as for his poetic genius).

Cortot belonged to the last generation for whom the piano itself was almost an object of worship, but though he loved it as much as any man, and understood all of its tonal resources, his use of it was always determined by a purely musical purpose. Beauty alone was never enough. It had to express something; it had to have meaning. At the same time, he was an unsurpassed master of characterization. In his hands, music emerged as intrinsically dramatic, continually responsive and developing. His rhythmic liberties were often extreme, and always inimitable, but they were never haphazard. Nor, simply because they were informed by a keen analytical mind, were they necessarily consistent. He recorded many works several times, and often revealed some fresh vision. For many people, Cortot had only one serious rival as a Chopin interpreter, and he could hardly have been more different.

Artur Rubinstein (1887–1982) – CD 2. Rubinstein was probably the most famous and certainly the most popular pianist of his time. His face, his name and playing were known in almost every country in the world. There were others whose fingers worked more infallibly, there were some (though not many) who could match the extent and the universality of his repertoire, and others whose intellects perhaps probed deeper, but no musician ever took or gave more sheer pleasure in the act of performance.

Gifted from birth with a natural facility and a prodigious memory, the young Rubinstein saw little virtue in practising. Indeed he saw little virtue in virtue. He was more interested in the easy pleasures of good wine, choice cigars and acquiescent women than in the pursuit of keyboard accuracy, and right up to the onset of middle age he regularly indulged his temperament at the expense of the notes.

As he approached his forties, Rubinstein was saddled (rightly, in his view) with the reputation of an ageing *Wunderkind* whose self-evident talent remained essentially unfocused and undisciplined. In 1932, all that changed. He settled down for the first time in his life to a period of relentless hard work and unflinching self-examination. The results were notable not only in a markedly increased professionalism but in a new seriousness of purpose.

Rubinstein's temperament, lucidity and deep pianistic instinct found perhaps their most natural, and certainly their most famous fusion in the music of Chopin, as may be heard here in his wonderful 1928 recording of the great *Barcarolle* (regarded by many musicians as Chopin's finest work). Indeed he substantially altered the way in which Chopin was commonly regarded. Though not as single-handedly as he liked to make out, he was one of the first to challenge the exaggerated Romanticism that characterized the playing of most nineteenth-century pianists. Even as late as the 1920s his Chopin playing was thought by many critics to be unacceptably severe.

Rubinstein's playing differed from that of most pianists of the Romantic tradition in being entirely without mannerisms or idiosyncrasies of any kind. With a few extravagant exceptions, this was a hallmark of what might be described, admittedly simplistically, as the twentieth-century style, in which the glorification of the pianist, a central feature of Romanticism, was supplanted by a new submission to the dictates of the composer.

Benno Moiseiwitsch (1890–1963) – CD 2. When Moiseiwitsch was born, in Russia, Liszt was only recently dead, Anton Rubinstein was still very much alive, and Paderewski was in his prime. By the time he left Russia, 15 years later, Moiseiwitsch was a seasoned prodigy with a burgeoning ego and a marked dislike of practising. Then he went for lessons with the great Leschetizky in Vienna. Having tossed off with supreme confidence a performance of Chopin's 'Revolutionary' Étude, the young genius turned to the old master in the full, and by now habitual, expectation of approval. 'I can play better than that,' said Leschetizky, 'with my left foot. There are at least a hundred delicate nuances in that piece which you have sacrificed simply for the effect you can make. I'm not interested in exhibitionism. Go away and practise decently for a couple of months until you've mastered real control. Then come back and we'll see what can be done.'

From that day forward, Moiseiwitsch became a tireless worker. He acquired a control of his instrument which has rarely been surpassed and developed into a thoughtful, essentially introspective musician for whom playing the piano seemed as effortless as breathing. No less remarkable than his dexterity was his flowing rhythm and the quick-silver delicacy of his tone. He was never a flamboyant player. The music always came first and he claimed to see himself as little more than a medium. But he also had the old-fashioned Romantic's extreme self-confidence. In 1915 he made his first recording, of Ravel's *Jeux d'eau*. Shortly afterwards he met the composer, who had both heard and admired the performance. 'There is just one thing, though,' said Ravel. 'In one place you slow up where I haven't indicated that you should.' 'But what you wrote,' replied Moiseiwitsch, '*requires* a ritard. If you didn't want a ritard there you should have written something else.' Ravel conceded the point.

Arturo Benedetti Michelangeli (1920–95) – CD 2. Michelangeli came as close to pianistic infallibility as mere mortals have been allowed to get. It seems unlikely that he played more than a dozen wrong notes in his entire career. A colourist in a million, his playing was nevertheless criticized in some circles for its coldness and aloofness, one great musician describing him witheringly as the 'Great Mortician'. He was notorious for his last-minute cancellations and his severely restricted public repertoire – barely more than a dozen works, including, most famously, Ravel's *Gaspard de la Nuit* and G major Concerto, the Bach–Busoni Chaconne, Rachmaninov's seldom championed Fourth Piano Concerto and, as can be heard here, the Brahms *Paganini Variations*, which for some reason he played in an order of his own devising.

Further Reading

Of books for the committed pianophile, pride of place must go to
Arthur Loesser's classic *Men, Women & Pianos* (New York, 1954).
Slightly in excess of 650 pages, this vastly informative and often
entertaining book is preponderantly a social history but nevertheless
contains enough technical information on the evolution of the instrument to satisfy any but the most case-hardened doctoral candidate.
The author himself was a pianist and teacher of enormous distinction,
and a man whose culture was as wide as his scholarship was deep.
Some readers may find his persistent cynicism a little tiresome after a
while, and there are certainly moments when his cleverness is too
clever by half, but the book is valuable far beyond the number of its
irritants, though it has no illustrations – a regrettable lapse which is
more than made up for by *The Book of the Piano*, edited by Dominic
Gill (Oxford, 1981), perhaps the most lavishly illustrated and wide-
ranging book on the subject ever printed. The writing, while never
less than authoritative, is uneven in quality and often more informative
than genuinely enlightening, but the pictures are well worth the price
of admission. Readers desirous of more concision can turn also to *The
Piano* in the New Grove Musical Instruments Series (London, 1980,
rev. 1988). A relatively brief, unimaginatively illustrated survey, this
symposium draws on the expertise of nine contributors, all eminent in
their field, and can better be recommended as a source of information
than as an absorbing read.

More specialized books on the subject fall generally into three
categories: those concerned with the history and marketing of the
instrument itself, those dealing primarily with repertoire and interpretation, and those devoted to pianists themselves. Among the first
group, two in particular can be strongly recommended. Rosamond
E. M. Harding's pioneering work, *The Pianoforte: Its History Traced to
the Great Exhibition of 1851* (London, 1933, rev. 1978) is indispensable to

the serious student of pianistic history. Crammed with information and written in an attractively accessible style, it nevertheless contains far more mechanical detail than the casually interested reader may care to sift through. Much the same can be said of Professor Cyril Ehrlich's painstaking study, *The Piano: A History* (Oxford, 1976, rev. 1990). Essential to the serious scholar, it may well intimidate the lay reader with its pervasive emphasis on statistics and marketing history, but it remains a work of distinguished scholarship and is by no means without its entertaining moments.

Although distinctly dated, and variable in accuracy, *Pianos and Their Makers* by Alfred Dolge (Covina, 1911, reissued by Dover in 1972) is a mine of information and incidental insights, and has a sense of immediacy not evident in many more scholarly tomes by outsiders (the author himself was one of the great figures in the piano industry, specializing in felts and soundboards).

Of books devoted specifically to performers, *The Great Pianists* by Harold C. Schonberg (New York, 1963) has become something of a classic. An absorbing survey, packed with information, anecdotes, good quotations and a wide first-hand knowledge of the subject, Schonberg's book is more journalistic than scholarly, and his division of pianists into various national schools is sometimes a little simplistic, but this need not detract from a thoroughly good read. Abram Chasins's *Speaking of Pianists* (New York, 1957, rev. 1973) is narrower in scope but an excellent example of enlightened gossip. A wide-ranging mixture of anecdote, portraiture and personal observation, this book by an accomplished pianist, composer and highly opinionated critic is confined to those pianists of whose playing the author had first-hand experience, from Paderewski to Gould. Harvey Sachs's *Virtuoso* (London, 1982) is another fascinating gallery of critical portraits. Finally, two interesting collections of interviews: *Great Pianists Speak for Themselves* by Elyse Mach (London, 1981) and David Dubal's *The World of the Concert Pianist* (London, 1985), both of which are full of stimulating surprises.

Further Listening

In a category of unlimited scope, where does one begin? Perhaps with artists, and with branches of the repertoire, regretfully omitted from the main text. No library of great piano records should be without the complete recordings of Rachmaninov, made between 1919 and 1942, or the complete solo recordings of Ignaz Friedman, made between 1923 and 1936. Friedman's way with Chopin's Mazurkas was unique and quite inimitable; his playing of Chopin's late E flat Nocturne is one of the greatest performances ever set down, as is his bewitching account of Mendelssohn's F sharp minor Venetian Boat Song from the *Songs without Words*. The great but erratic Wilhelm Kempff's recording of his own transcriptions of Bach, Handel, Mozart and Gluck is one of the most bewitchingly beautiful and pianistically sophisticated records ever made. Claudio Arrau's traversal of the Chopin Nocturnes contains some of the greatest playing he ever did, ditto Sviatoslav Richter's incandescent account of Debussy's *Pagodes* – one of the true miracles of modern pianism. Richter also turns up trumps with his staggering illumination of Mussorgsky's *Pictures at an Exhibition* (so does Horowitz) and his recording of Liszt's *Feux Follets* is probably unequalled. Horowitz's concert performance of the Tchaikovsky First Concerto with Toscanini is in a class by itself, but if you want a more modern recording Emil Gilels, Martha Argerich, Van Cliburn and Earl Wild all turn in superb performances. Richter in the Rachmaninov Second Concerto is unsurpassed, so is Argerich in the Third. Nor has Cliburn's Moscow recording of Rachmaninov's B flat minor Sonata been bettered. Anton Kuerti's disc of Russian music is likewise of the very highest quality, especially his dazzling and impeccably idiomatic playing of Glazunov's Concert Waltz in E flat. Listeners wanting to explore the Spanish repertoire, dominated by Albéniz, Granados and Falla, can safely rely on Alicia de Larrocha but should also seek out any of Artur Rubinstein's early Spanish discs, or, going back still further in time, those of Ricardo Viñes (whose Debussy playing, too, is of sovereign quality). Harold Bauer, one of the most inexplicably neglected pianists in history, made some of the best piano records ever issued in the 1920s and 1930s, and his magnificent playing of Beethoven's 'Moonlight' and 'Appassionata' Sonatas is equalled by his account of Brahms's F minor Sonata.

Chronology

DATE	MILESTONE	MUSICAL CONTEXT	HISTORICAL BACKGROUND
1709	Cristofori builds the first piano.	Handel's opera *Agrippina* produced in Venice. Bach composes much organ music.	Marlborough defeats French at Malplaquet. Peter the Great defeats Charles XII in Battle of Poltava.
1711	Maffei publishes first detailed account of Cristofori's invention.	Clarinet used for the first time in orchestra. Handel's *Rinaldo* performed in London.	Steele and Addison found the *Spectator*. Invention of the tuning fork. Queen Anne establishes Ascot races in England.
1725	Maffei's article published in German in Mattheson's *Critica musica*.	First public concerts given in Paris. J. J. Fux's treaty on counterpoint, *Gradus ad Parnassum*. A. Scarlatti dies.	Death of Peter the Great. Treaty of Vienna guarantees Pragmatic Sanction. Louis XV marries Maria Leszczynska of Poland.
1742	Earliest known square piano built by Johann Söcher.	Handel's *Messiah* first performed. Karl Graun introduces Italian opera to Berlin.	Celsius invents centigrade thermometer. Resignation of Walpole, chief minister in Britain for 21 years.
1763	Piano first played in public in Vienna.	Birth of composers Méhul and Gyrowetz.	Peace of Paris ends Seven Years' War. Indian uprising near Detroit spreads eastwards. Boswell meets Johnson.
1768	Thomas Walsh plays the first public solo on the piano in Dublin; J. C. Bach follows suit in London.	Mozart (12) composes his first operas, *La Finta semplice*, and *Bastien und Bastienne* which is produced in Vienna.	*Encyclopaedia Britannica* begun. Royal Academy of Arts founded in London. Massachusetts Assembly petitions against taxation without representation. Captain Cook's first Pacific voyage (to 1771).
1773	Piano makes its solo debut in America.	The waltz becomes fashionable in Paris.	Boston Tea Party.
1776			American Declaration of Independence.
1781	Broadwood in London builds his first grand. Pianistic 'duel' between Mozart and Clementi.	Haydn publishes his 'Russian' Quartets. Mozart's *Idomeneo* produced in Munich.	Emperor Joseph II abolishes serfdom and grants religious toleration. Kant: *Critique of Pure Reason*. Herschel discovers planet Uranus. First building societies in Britain. First iron bridge opened at Coalbrookdale.
1783	Broadwood moves wrest plank to back of case, improves dampers and replaces Zumpe's hand stops with 'loud' and 'soft' pedals.	Beethoven's first works printed. Mozart composes his Mass in C minor.	Potëmkin conquers Crimea for Russia. First ascent in hot-air balloon. Invention of the paddle-wheel steamer.
1789			French Revolution, followed by Reign of Terror (1793–4) and war in Europe (1792–1815).
1795	William Stodart of London effectively up-ends grand piano to create the first upright.	Haydn completes 'London' Symphonies. Paris Conservatoire founded.	Rule of Directory begins in France. First horse-drawn railway in England.
1796	Erard in Paris builds his first grand.	Beethoven composes Cello Sonatas (op. 5).	Death of Catherine the Great of Russia. Edward Jenner introduces vaccination against smallpox.

DATE	MILESTONE	MUSICAL CONTEXT	HISTORICAL BACKGROUND
1802	Thomas Loud introduces overstringing.	Beethoven composes Symphony no. 2.	Napoleon becomes First Consul for life. Peace of Amiens.
1808	Broadwood introduces metal tension bars to grand. Erard patents his 'repetition action' and introduces 'agraffe'.	Beethoven's Symphonies no. 5 and no. 6 ('Pastoral') composed.	US prohibits importation of slaves from Africa. French occupy Rome and invade Spain.
1811	Wornum builds his first 'cottage piano'.	Franz Liszt born. Beethoven's 'Emperor' Concerto.	George III of Great Britain pronounced insane: Regency begins. Luddites sabotage machinery in Britain. Jane Austen's *Sense and Sensibility* published.
1821	Erard patents his revolutionary 'double escapement' action.	Weber: *Der Freischütz*. Beethoven: Piano Sonatas op. 110 and 111.	Death of Napoleon. Death of Keats. First steps in sound reproduction. Scott: *Kenilworth*.
1825	Babcock patents cast-iron frame for square piano. Courcel's 'Cylindrichord' anticipates player piano.	Johann Strauss the Younger born. Schubert composes A minor Sonata D845, D major Sonata D850 and Ninth Symphony.	Accession of Nicholas I in Russia. First Baseball Club at Rochester, NY. Stockton–Darlington railway opened (first to be designed for steam locomotives). Constable: *The Haywain*.
1826	Pape patents felt-covered hammers.	Mendelssohn (17) composes Overture to *A Midsummer Night's Dream*. Weber dies at 40.	Thomas Jefferson dies. First railway tunnel in Britain. Munich University and University College, London founded.
1832	First Canadian piano built.	Donizetti: *L'elisir d'amore*. Clementi dies.	Reform bill passed by British Parliament. Mazzini founds 'Young Italy' movement.
1837			Accession of Queen Victoria.
1839	Liszt gives first ever solo piano recital.	Berlioz' *Roméo et Juliette* first performed. Chopin: 24 Preludes (op. 28).	First Opium War. Chartist Convention in London. Bicycle invented. Turner: *The Fighting Téméraire*.
1840	Chickering unveils his improved cast-iron frame for uprights.	Chopin's op. 35–42 published. Schumann writes over 100 songs. Saxophone invented.	Penny Post in Britain. Poe: *Tales of the Grotesque and Arabesque*. Dickens: *The Old Curiosity Shop*.
1848–9			'Year of Revolutions' in Europe.
1851	Chickering exhibits cast-iron frame for grands.	Verdi's *Rigoletto* produced in Venice.	Louis Napoleon's *coup d'état* in France. Great Exhibition in London. *New York Times* established. Singer designs continuous-stitch sewing machine. Double-decker bus introduced in London.
1853	Steinway, Bechstein and Blüthner established.	Verdi's *Il Trovatore* and *La Traviata* produced.	Crimean War begins (to 1856). End of transportation of English criminals to New South Wales. First railway through the Alps. Dickens: *Bleak House*.
1855	Steinway introduces overstrung square piano.	Berlioz' *Te Deum* first performed.	Livingstone discovers Victoria Falls. Tennyson: *Maud*.

DATE	MILESTONE	MUSICAL CONTEXT	HISTORICAL BACKGROUND
1859	Steinway patents overstrung grand.	Brahms premières his D minor Concerto (no. 1). Gounod's *Faust* first performed. Wagner completes *Tristan and Isolde*.	Austrians defeated at Battle of Solferino by the French and Sardinians. George Eliot: *Adam Bede*. Charles Darwin: *The Origin of Species*.
1861			American Civil War begins. Victor Emmanuel first king of a united Italy. Emancipation of the serfs in Russia.
1862	Montal invents the 'sostenuto' pedal which later becomes standard issue on all grand pianos.	Debussy born. Berlioz' opera *Béatrice et Bénédict* produced in Germany. Verdi's *La Forza del Destino* produced in Russia.	Bismarck becomes chief minister of Prussia. English cricket team tours Australia for the first time. Hugo: *Les Misérables*.
1863	Steinway patents fan-like overstringing. First fully automated pneumatic piano built.	Bizet's *Les Pêcheurs de perles* produced. First production of Berlioz' opera *Les Troyens*.	President Lincoln issues Emancipation Proclamation, freeing all American slaves. First Impressionist works exhibited in Paris. London Underground opens.
1867	Triumph of 'American system' at Paris Exhibition.	Johann Strauss composes *The Blue Danube* waltz. Verdi's *Don Carlos* produced in Paris. Brahms: *German Requiem*.	Austro-Hungarian Dual Monarchy established. Karl Marx: *Das Kapital*. Game of Badminton invented in Britain. Earliest recorded bicycle race in France. Lister performs first antiseptic operation.
1878	First Japanese piano unveiled in Paris.	Gilbert and Sullivan's *H.M.S. Pinafore* produced.	Electric street lighting introduced in London. Microphone invented. First commercial production of Edison's phonograph.
1887	Yamaha founded in Japan.	Verdi: *Otello*. Brahms: Concerto for Violin and Cello.	Queen Victoria celebrates her Golden Jubilee. Existence of radio waves demonstrated by Hertz. Berliner patents the gramophone.
1904	Welte unveils his *Mignon*, the first really viable reproducing piano.	Puccini's *Madame Butterfly* produced in Milan. Janáček's *Jenůfa* produced in Brno. Dvořák dies.	Theodore Roosevelt President of US. Russo-Japanese War (to 1905). Chekhov: *The Cherry Orchard*. Trans-Siberian railway completed. First telegraphic transmission of photographs.
1913	Introduction of the two most successful reproducing systems. The American Duo-Art and Ampico.	Stravinsky's *Rite of Spring* causes riot in Paris. Falla's *La vida breve* produced in France. Debussy's ballet *Jeux* performed in Paris.	Suffragette demonstrations in London. Federal Income Tax introduced in the USA. Woodrow Wilson becomes US President. War in the Balkans enters second year.
1914–18			First World War.
1917		Prokofiev: *Classical Symphony*. Ravel: *Le Tombeau de Couperin*.	Bolshevik Revolution in Russia.

DATE	MILESTONE	MUSICAL CONTEXT	HISTORICAL BACKGROUND
1925	Kawai founded in Japan.	Berg's *Wozzeck* produced in Berlin.	Fitzgerald: *The Great Gatsby*. The Bauhaus founded by Walter Gropius. Eisenstein: *The Battleship Potĕmkin*.
1933	Advent of the electric piano with the Neo-Bechstein.	Richard Strauss' *Arabella* produced in Dresden. Copland writes *Short Symphony*.	Hitler becomes German Chancellor; Third Reich formed. Franklin Roosevelt elected US President.
1940	John Cage produces his first works for 'prepared' piano.	Shostakovich composes Seventh Symphony. Stravinsky writes Symphony in C. Britten composes *Sinfonia da Requiem*.	World War II enters second year. Trotsky assassinated in Mexico.
1969	Japan becomes the world's largest piano manufacturer.	Stockhausen: *Stimmung*. Berio: *Sinfonia*. Tippett: *The Knot Garden*.	Nixon becomes US President. Golda Meir becomes Israeli Prime Minister. Czech federal government suppressed by USSR. First landing on the moon.

Acknowledgements

The Publishers gratefully acknowledge permission given by the following to reproduce illustrations and photographs: Steinway & Sons Collection, LaGuardia and Wagner Archives, LaGuardia Community College/CUNY 1; Copyright © The Metropolitan Museum of Art, The Crosby Brown Collection of Musical Instruments, 1889. (89.4.1219) 6; Stiftung Preussische Schlösser und Gärten Berlin-Brandenburg 11; Yale Center for British Art, Paul Mellon Collection 17; Mary Evans Picture Library 18, 55, 60, 69, 80, 82, 105, 139, 142, 151 (from the *Illustrated London News*, 5 July, 1851), 159, 163; The Board of Trustees of The Victoria & Albert Museum, London 25; Copyright © The Metropolitan Museum of Art, Gift of Helen C. Lanier, 1981. (1981.477) 27; Smithsonian Institution Photo No. 56,414 28, Photo No. 56,414A 29, Photo No. 78–12539 88, Photo No. 76–19238 91, Photo No. 56378B 153; AKG London 30; AKG London (Körner-Museum, Dresden) 31; Royal College of Music 32, 58, 62; AKG London (Royal College of Music, London) 37; AKG London/Photo Erich Lessing 39; AKG London/ Photo Erich Lessing (Historisches Museum der Stadt Wien) 42 and 43; Historisches Museum der Stadt Wien 44; Sotheby's 45; The Metropolitan Museum of Art, The Crosby Brown Collection of Musical Instruments, 1889. (89.4.2804) 46; Copyright © The Metropolitan Museum of Art, Gift of Mrs. Henry McSweeny, 1959. (59.76) 48; Mansell Collection 49; Collection Haags Gemeentemuseum 1996 c/o Beeldrecht Amstelveen 50; Corbis-Bettmann 54, 110, 112; Musée de la ville de Paris, Musée Carnavalet/Lauros-Giraudon 65; AKG London/Photo Erich Lessing (Sammlung Bösendorfer, Vienna) 67; Bibliothèque Polonaise, Paris/Photo © Patrick Lorette-Giraudon 71; Bibliotcka Jagicllonska, Cracow 72; Bibliothèque Nationale, Paris/Lauros-Giraudon 73; Angelo Agostini, *A Vide Fluminense*, 2 October 1869 76; Collection S. Frederick Starr 79; Steinway & Sons 85, 123; Bibliothèque Inguimbertine, Carpentras/Lauros-Giraudon 89, 93; Mansell Collection 94; © Collection VIOLLET 95; H. Roger-Viollet 97; Christie's Images 101; Hulton Getty 109, 162; Culver Pictures 120, 122, 125, 150; Robert Morley & Co. Ltd., London 126; British Library, London (F 449) (from the *Illustrirte Zeitung*, Leipzig 1887) 127; Royal Society of Musicians/RCM 134; Musée des Beaux-Arts Jules Cheret, Nice/© ADAGP, Paris and DACS, London 1996 144; Peter Newark's Pictures 146; Germanisches Nationalmuseum, Nuremberg 147; The Illustrated London News Picture Library (from the *Illustrated London News*, 11 November 1922) 161.

Index